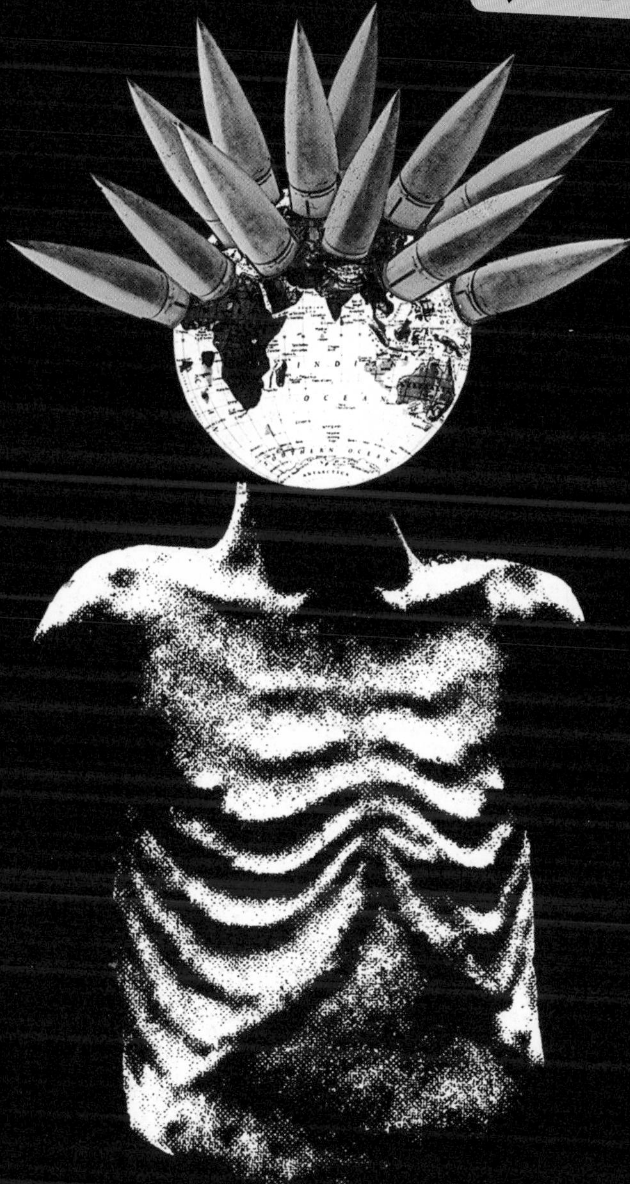

This book was made with Kam Rehal, and my sons Daniel and Matthew.
Thanks a lot.

Also, thanks to everyone at IWM who helped with the book especially Madeleine James, Kay Heather, Elizabeth Bowers, Kieran Whitworth and Richard Slocombe for his Introduction.

In memory of my great friend Al Rees, 1949–2014

Published by IWM, Lambeth Road, London SE1 6HZ
iwm.org.uk



ISBN 978-1-904897-71-2

A catalogue record for this book is available from the British Library.

Colour reproduction by DL Imaging
Printed by Graphicom on Cyclus Offset, a paper made from 100 per cent recycled fibre



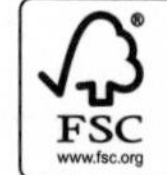
MIX
Paper from responsible sources
FSC® C013123

# INTRODUCTION

'A single death is a tragedy; a million deaths is a statistic'

This apocryphal statement was said to have been made by Soviet dictator Josef Stalin in 1943. Shocking in its blunt candidness, it nevertheless affirms the inability of the mind to process the scale of human suffering that is a hallmark of the last century. This is a book of similar statistics; bald, grim, real but unquantifiable. Together they present a harsh critique of today's world; one wracked with inequality, wealth disparity and skewed priorities, where basic human compassion is often trumped by corporate interests and the rivalry of richer nations.

Accompanying these statistics are images produced from 1968 to the present. They tackle half a century of conflict, including the Vietnam War, the Cold War and the nuclear arms race, the Gulf War, the break-up of Yugoslavia and the recent US-led invasions of Iraq and Afghanistan. Other images address numerous humanitarian issues, from the brutality of the Pinochet *junta* in Chile in the 1970s to the plight of Britain's homelessin the 1990s.

They are the work of one artist, Peter Kennard.

With a career spanning almost fifty years, Peter Kennard is without doubt Britain's most important political artist and its leading practitioner of photomontage. His adoption of the medium in the late 1960s restored an association with radical politics, and drew inspiration from the anti-Nazi montages of John Heartfield in the 1930s. Many of Kennard's images are now themselves icons of the medium, defining the tenor of protest in recent times and informing the subsequent visual culture of conflict and crisis in modern history.

Kennard defines his role as that of a 'communicator' and so is determined to make art that exists outside the confines of the art world, stating in 1990: 'For me, getting the work out into the world and used is as important as its production.'[1]

This has served as both maxim and method for Kennard and since the early 1970s he has brought his art to street-level, either as fly posters, protest placards or t-shirts in support of a variety of interest groups, including the Campaign for Nuclear Disarmament (CND) and Amnesty International.

Born in London in 1949, Kennard painted from the age of 13, using a coal shed as a makeshift studio. After securing a scholarship to attend Byam Shaw Art School in London he undertook further study at the Slade School of Art from 1967 to 1970 and at the Royal College of Art from 1976 to 1979.

It was at the Slade that Kennard underwent his political awakening. It was 1968; a momentous year when the world appeared convulsed in youthful insurrection against the status quo. The art he subsequently produced formed the basis of his career path, the artist recounting later:

> 'I studied as a painter, but after the events of 1968 I began to look for a form of expression that could bring art and politics together to a wider audience . . . I found however that photography wasn't as burdened with similar art historical associations.'[2]

[1] Kennard, Peter: *Images for the End of the Century: Photomontage Equations*, (1990), Journeyman Press, London

[2] Kennard, Peter: *Dispatches from an Unofficial War Artist*, (2000) Lund Humphries, Aldershot p.70

The result was Kennard's seminal *STOP* montage series. The 31 works, produced between 1968 and 1973, combined numerous, often iconic, photographs of contemporary events with a myriad of acetate overlays of abstract marks. By this, Kennard partly sought to replicate the disorientating atmosphere of the period as he experienced it himself as a student activist. The series also reflected his interest in the German poet and playwright Bertolt Brecht's theory of *Verfremdungseffekt* ('distancing effect'), whereby events are stripped of familiar attributes to create fresh curiosity and astonishment.

These powerful, experimental works, with their exploration of distorted perceptions and perspectives were typical of the dynamic milieu of the late 1960s. The dawning 1970s, however, brought simpler, starker imagery as Kennard's work assumed greater agitational force to raise awareness of human rights violations in Chile and Northern Ireland. These montages found a regular platform in the left-wing daily, *Workers' Press*, until disillusionment and editorial interference put paid to Kennard's involvement.

Kennard's work attained an early maturity in the 1980s amid the rising tensions of the Cold War and the divisive policies of Margaret Thatcher's Conservative administration. Simple, direct and often sardonic montages were made for CND, articulating fears inherent in British society as the stand-off between East and West pushed the world towards nuclear catastrophe. This culminated in Kennard's famous transposition of John Constable's *Haywain*, shown bristling with American cruise missiles in response to their deployment in Britain in 1982. On the strength of this imagery Ken Livingstone, then leader of the Greater London Council, commissioned Kennard in 1983 to give visual expression to his declaration of the capital as a 'nuclear-free zone'. *Target London*, a folio of 18 posters, bleakly satirised the Thatcher government's *Protect and Survive* nuclear attack directives and moved the critic Richard Cork to describe the series as the 'most hard-hitting attack on government imbecility'.[3]

In 1989 the fall of the Berlin Wall gave Kennard, like many, cause for hope. However the emergence of a new capitalistic global hegemony – the so-called 'new world order' – quickly dampened this initial optimism. The era heralded fresh artistic experimentation for the artist with the creation of a number of three-dimensional artworks. Kennard later explained these as arising from 'a mixture of personal experience, disillusion with organised politics and the use by the media of innumerable digital photomontages' causing him to 'question the effectiveness of photomontage as a critical, social probe'.[4]

Works such as *Welcome to Britain* (1995), an installation of placards and crates at the Royal Festival Hall, and *Reading Room* (1997), an arrangement of newspaper lecterns shown originally at Gimpel Fils Gallery, contemplated aspects of the developing post-Cold War, pre-millennium society, from Britain's dispossessed and homeless to the supremacy of the stock markets.

The outbreak of the Iraq War in 2003 caused Kennard to reconnect with photomontage. Working in collaboration with Cat Phillipps, they used digital technology to create one of the

[3] 'Peter Kennard' by Richard Cork for *The Listener* (8 August 1985) published in Cork, Richard: *New Spirit, New Sculpture, New Money: Art in the 1980s*, (2003) Yale University Press, London and New Haven

[4] Kennard, Peter: *Dispatches from an Unofficial War Artist*, p.35

archetypal images of the conflict. *Photo Op* (2005), picturing a grinning British Prime Minister Tony Blair posing for a selfie against a background inferno, has since become visual shorthand for the Blair administration's controversial policy in Iraq. Before this work Kennard created his *Decoration* (2003–2004) paintings, a grand series of eighteen three-metre high canvases which drew attention to the human cost of the Iraq War while simultaneously meditating on established tokens of commemoration and military valour. Generated by a combination of digital printing and oil paint, the *Decoration* series' concern with surface and finish also signalled Kennard's desire to connect with his first love of painting. This too was emphasised by his series, *Face* (2002–2003), a group of 28 anonymous portraits, which, merging in and out of darkness, stood for the voiceless and marginalised in a fragmented world.

Both series reveal the more contemplative nature of Kennard's mature work. Now entering his later career the artist has had cause for reflection on an *oeuvre* dedicated to the political and social causes of a turbulent half-century. This has inspired his latest work, *Boardroom*, an installation dwelling on aspects of modern conflict which incorporates some of his most familiar images and motifs. Interspersed among these are the same incomprehensible statistics that feature in this book.

*Boardroom* will debut at IWM London as part of the museum's retrospective exhibition of Kennard's work, *Peter Kennard: Unofficial War Artist*, in May 2015. This is just the latest chapter in a long association between artist and museum. Since the 1980s IWM has recognised Kennard's importance as an artist and commentator on the major conflicts of the day. His work's unerring ability to command the zeitgeist and resonate with many of the British public has seen it actively collected by the Department of Art. This has included the acquisition of original montages from Kennard's *Target London* series in the 1990s, followed by the purchase of nine works from the seminal *STOP* series in 2009. The contemporary significance of kennardphillipps's *Photo Op* was also quickly understood by IWM, resulting in the purchase of an image ahead of any other national collection.

Prior to this, in 1990 IWM also hosted a major exhibition of Kennard's work, *Images for the End of the Century*. The show reflected on the first twenty years of the artist's career, taking in work that contrasted the nuclear arms race with the plight of the Third World and the West's expedient support of brutal dictatorships. These works and Kennard himself looked too, with some hope, to the post-Cold War world, embodied in the fall of the Berlin Wall a year previously. The current exhibition at IWM will address the subsequent twenty years and provide extended analysis of the output and outlook of his life's work, so providing the fullest consideration of Peter Kennard – this unique, provocative and restlessly inventive British artist.

**Richard Slocombe**
*Senior Curator*, IWM

# WE ARE PEOPLES OF THE UNITED NATIONS DETERMINED

to save succeeding generations
from the scourge of war . . .

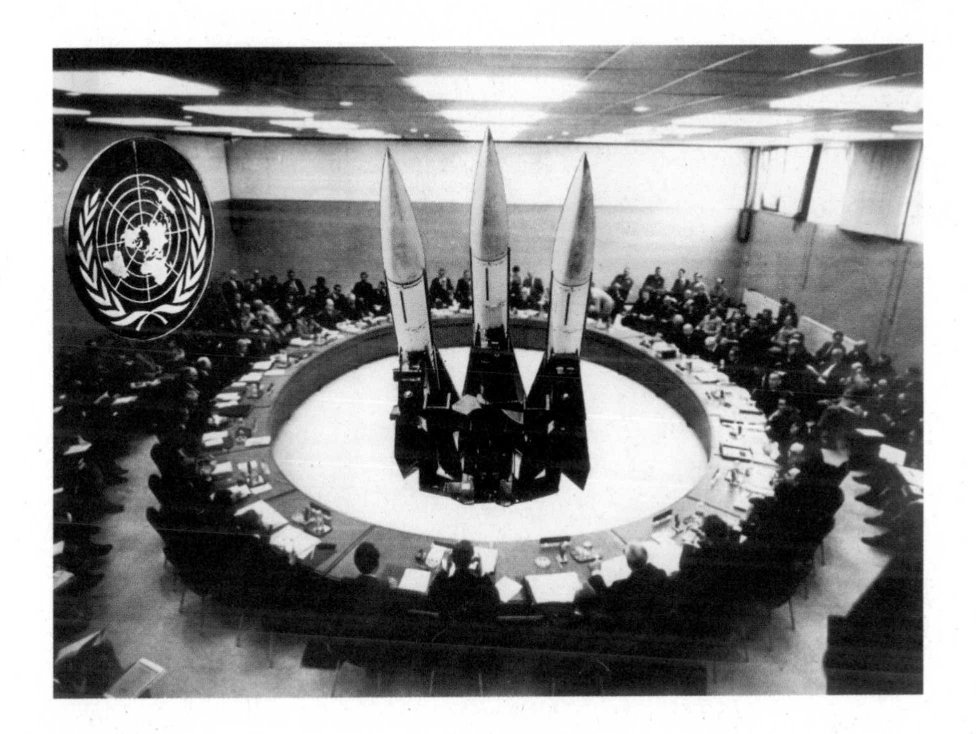

CHARTER OF THE UNITED NATIONS
Signed 26 June 1945

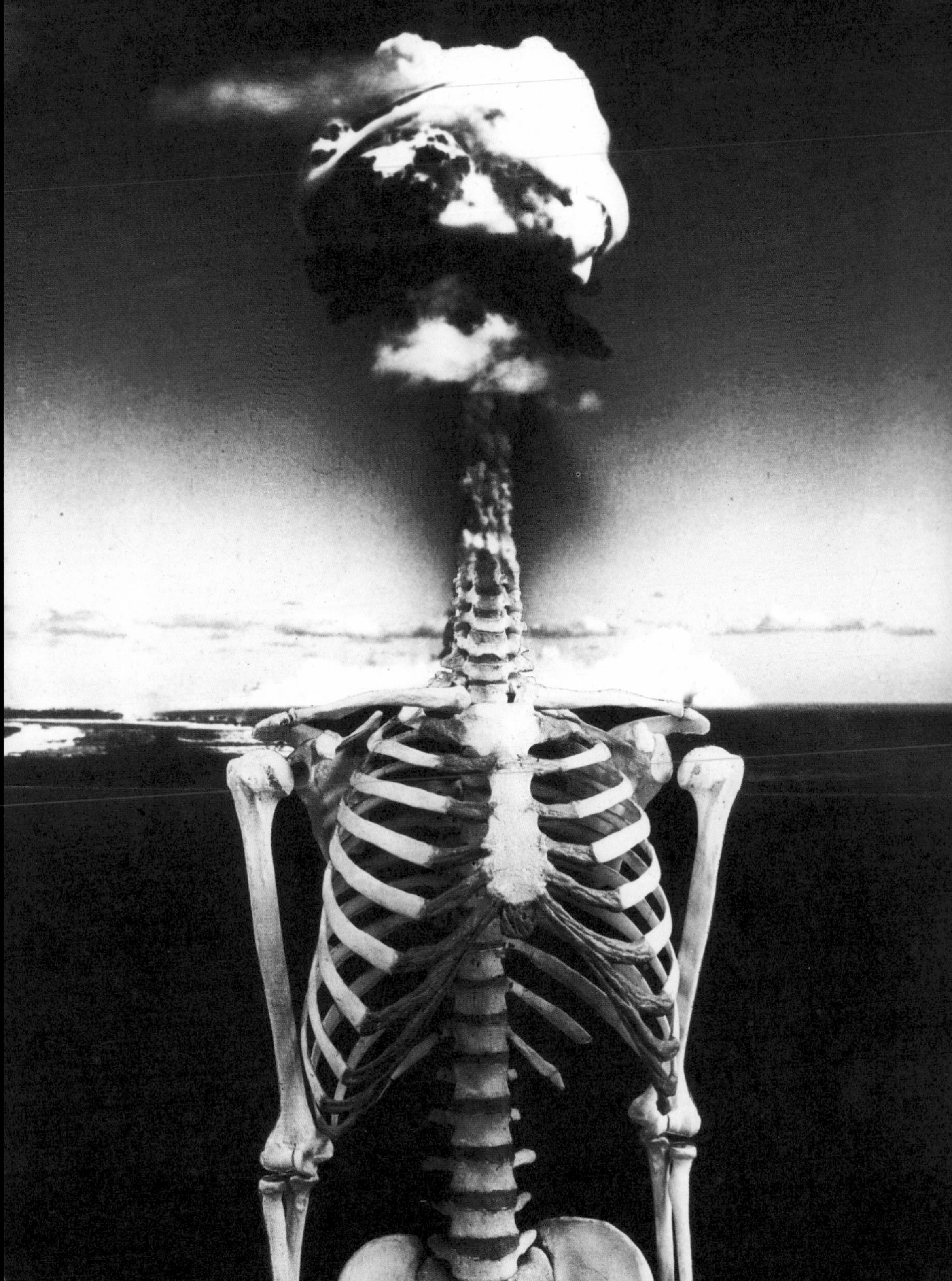

816

This watch stopped at 8.16am, the moment the atomic bomb exploded

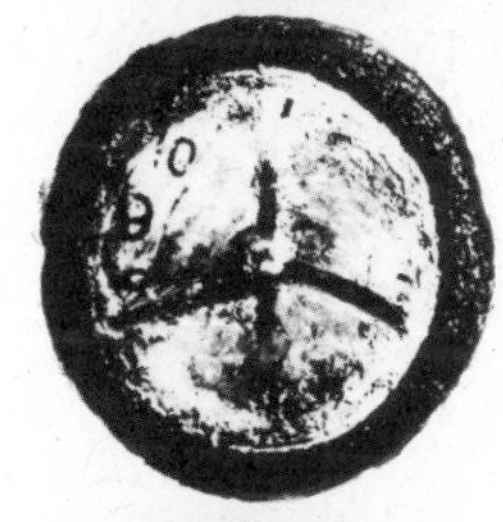

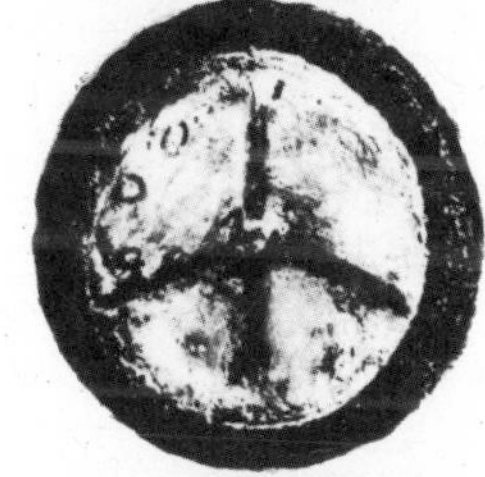

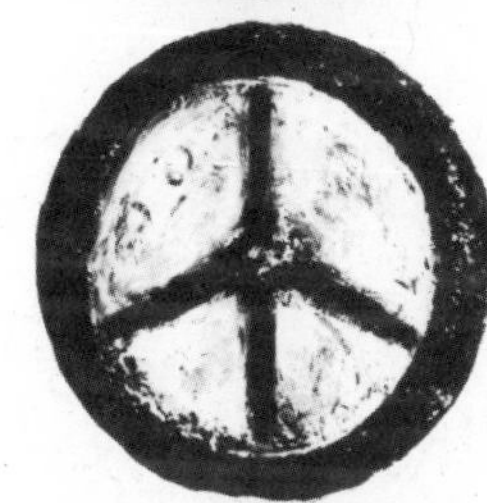

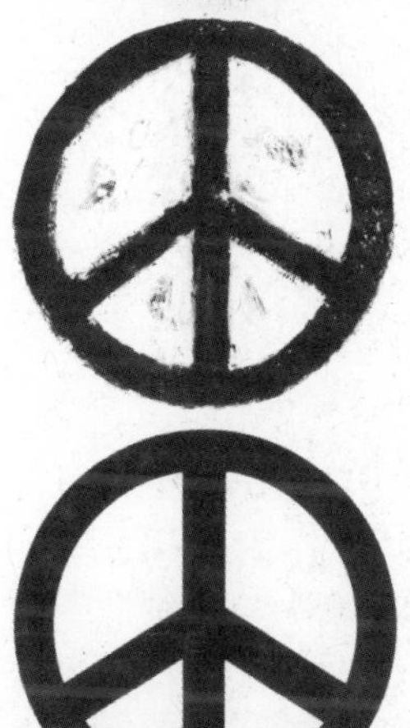

# 140000

On 6 August 1945, 140,000 people died when the atomic bomb was dropped on Hiroshima

Hiroshima Peace Memorial Museum

# 5

The five permanent members of the United Nations Security Council – UK, USA, Russia, China and France – are also the five largest arms traders in the world

Amnesty International

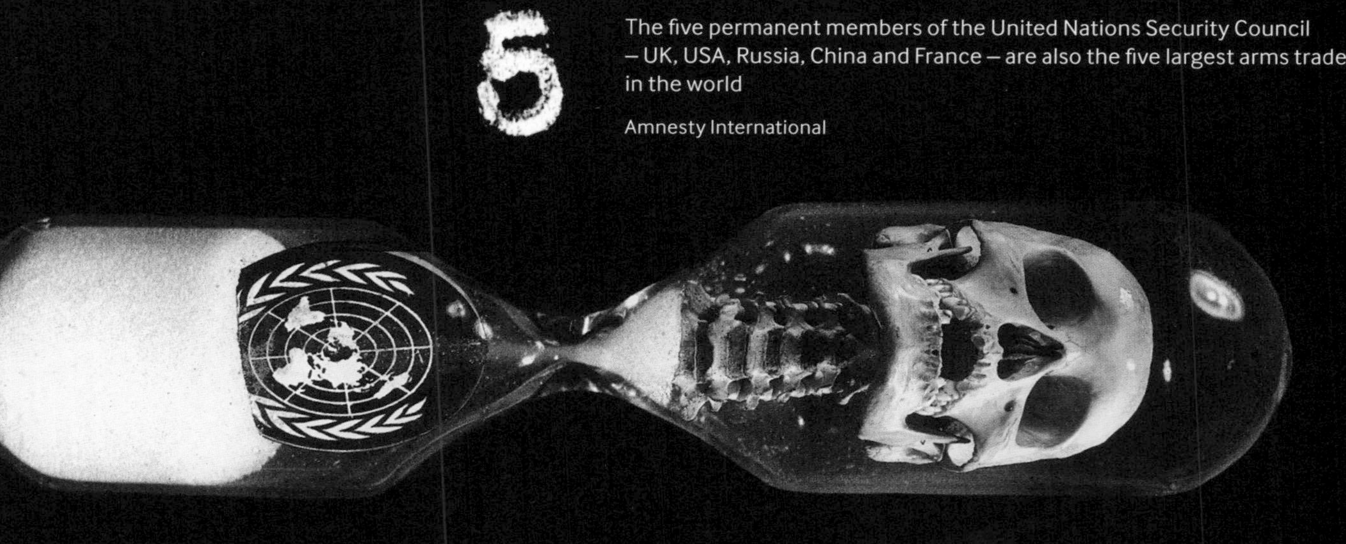

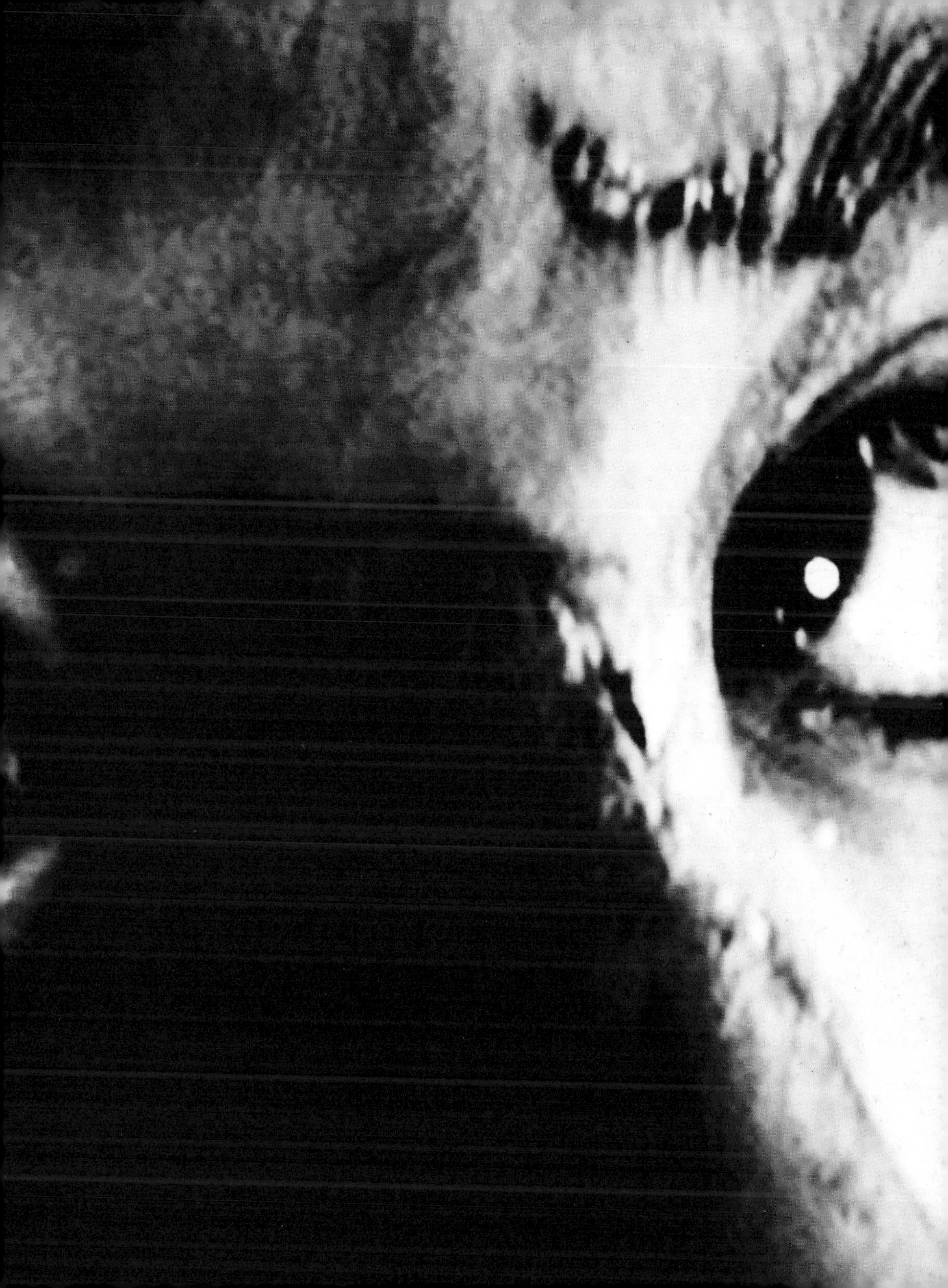

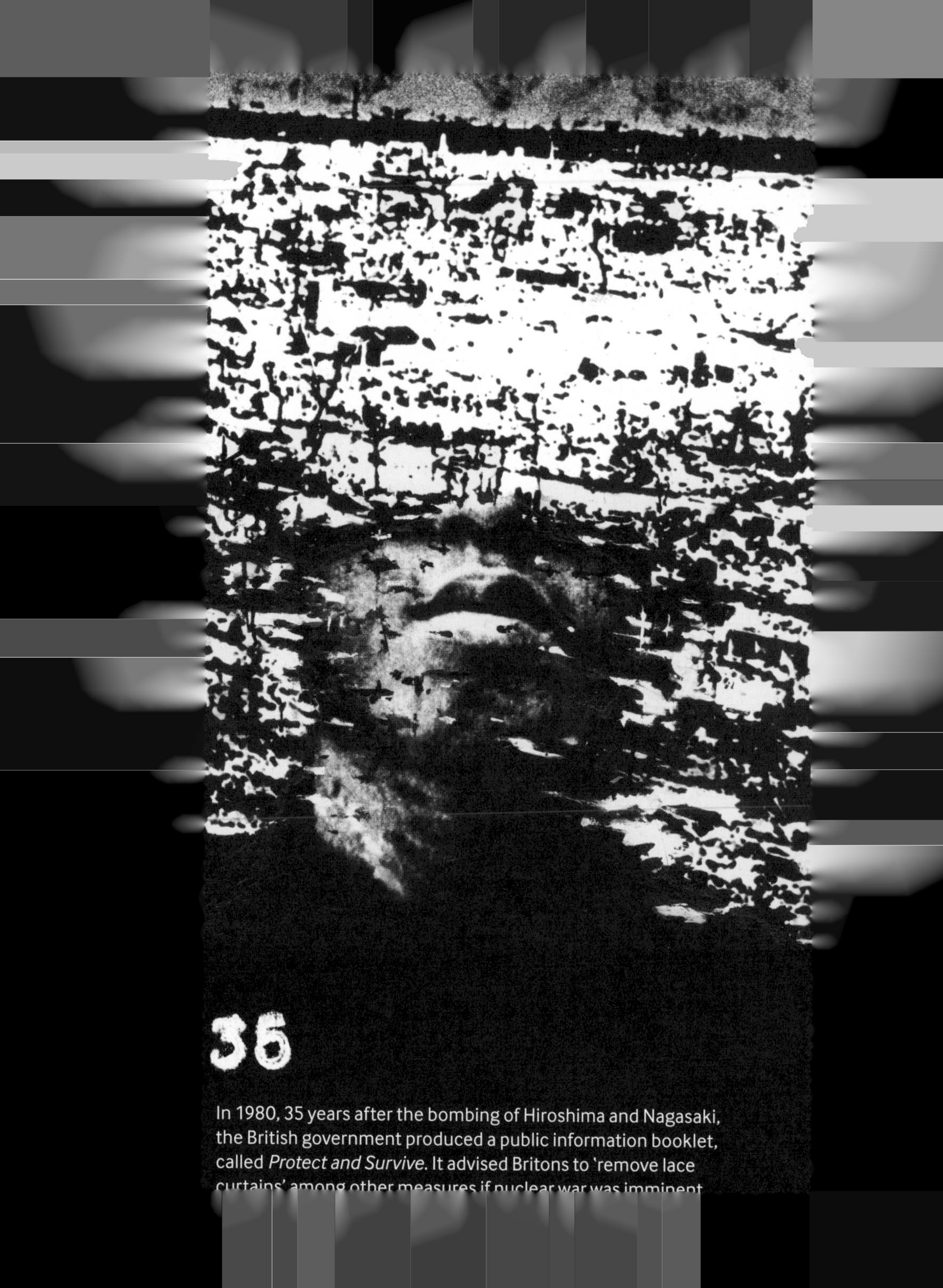

# 35

In 1980, 35 years after the bombing of Hiroshima and Nagasaki, the British government produced a public information booklet, called *Protect and Survive*. It advised Britons to 'remove lace curtains' among other measures if nuclear war was imminent.

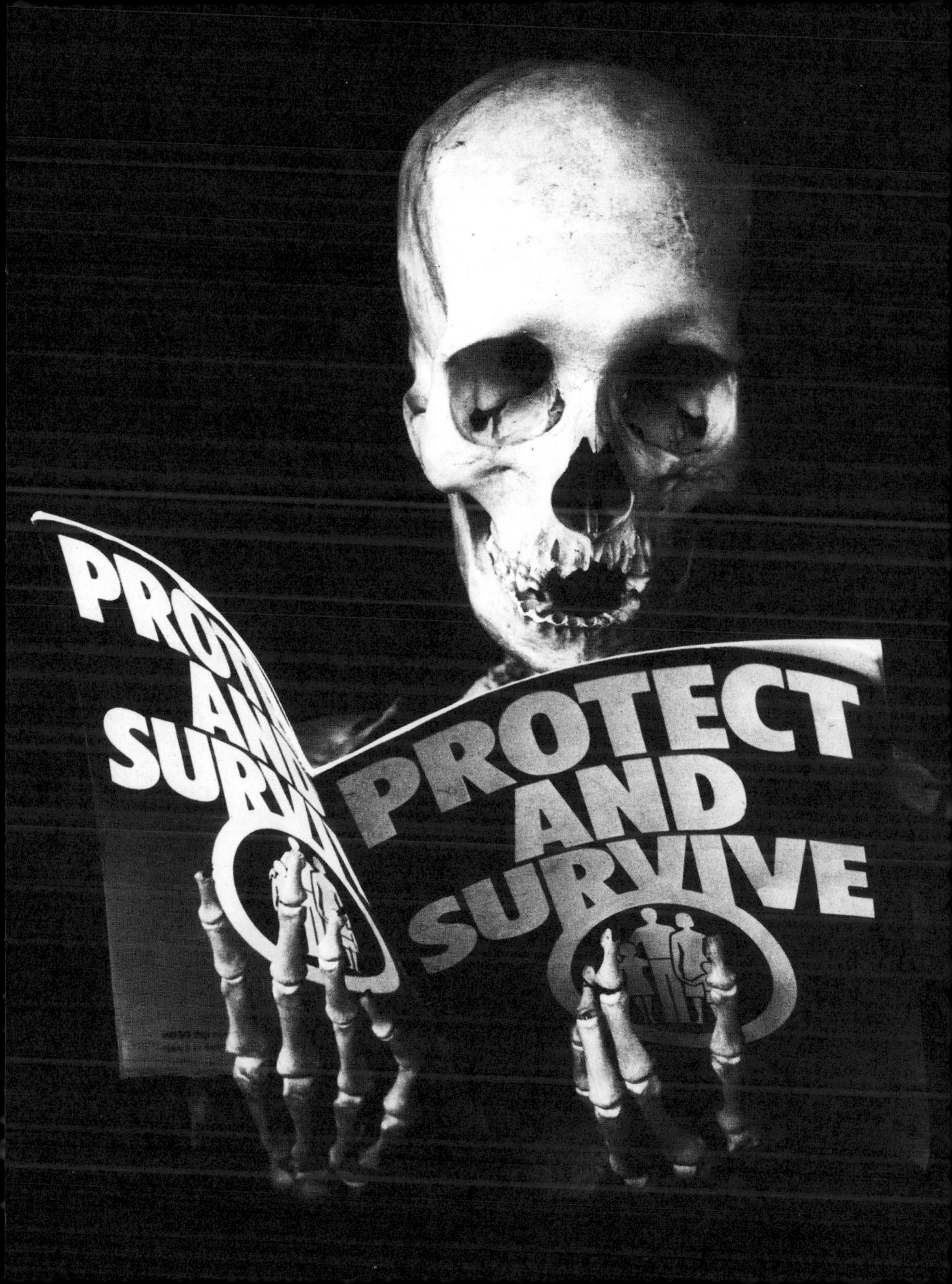

PROTECT
AND
SURVIVE

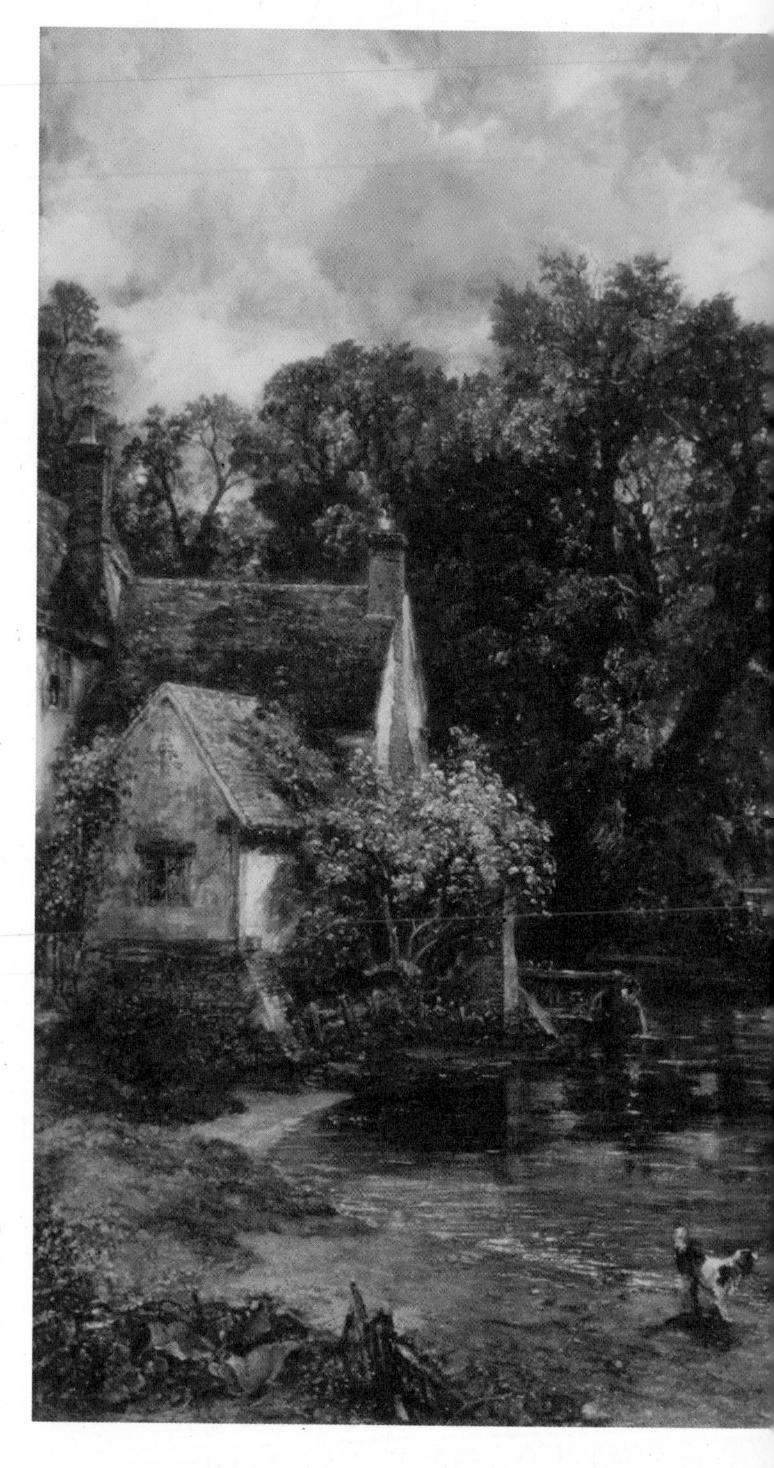

# 662

The US has 662 reported military bases around the world

US Department of Defense, 2010

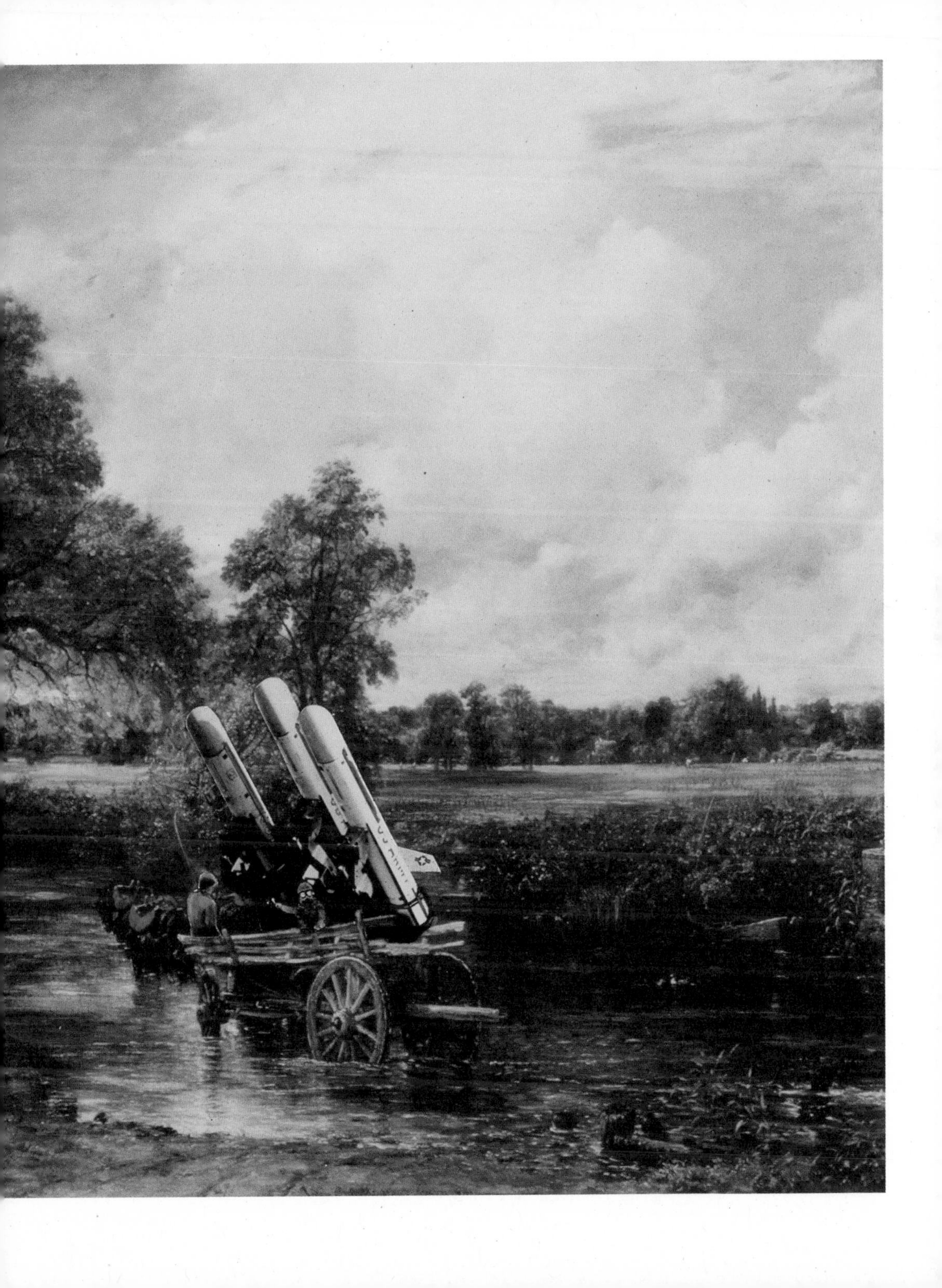

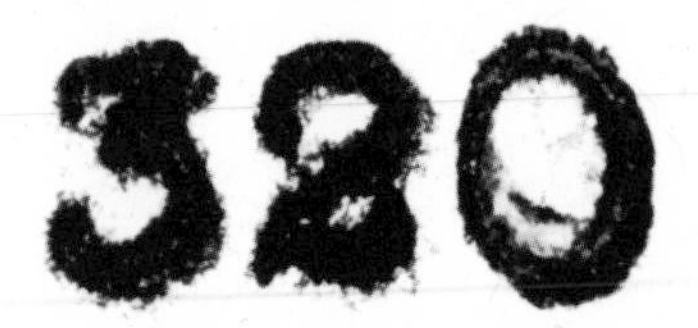


The explosive power of the nuclear weapons carried on each of the four British Trident submarines is equal to 320 Hiroshima bombs

Campaign for Nuclear Disarmament

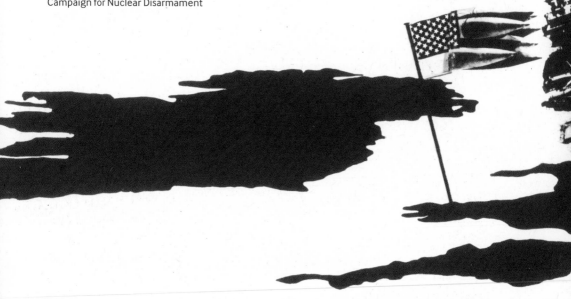

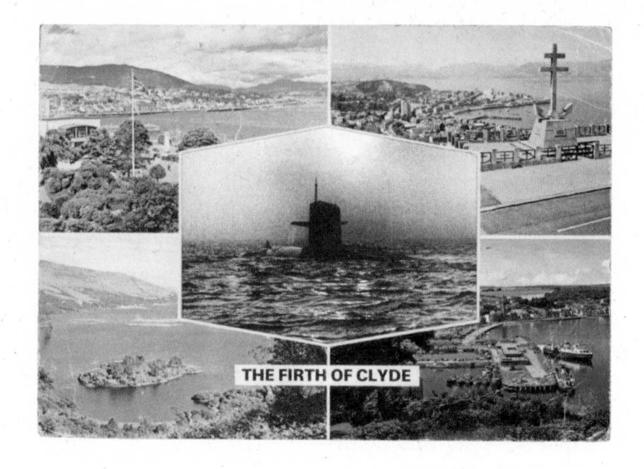

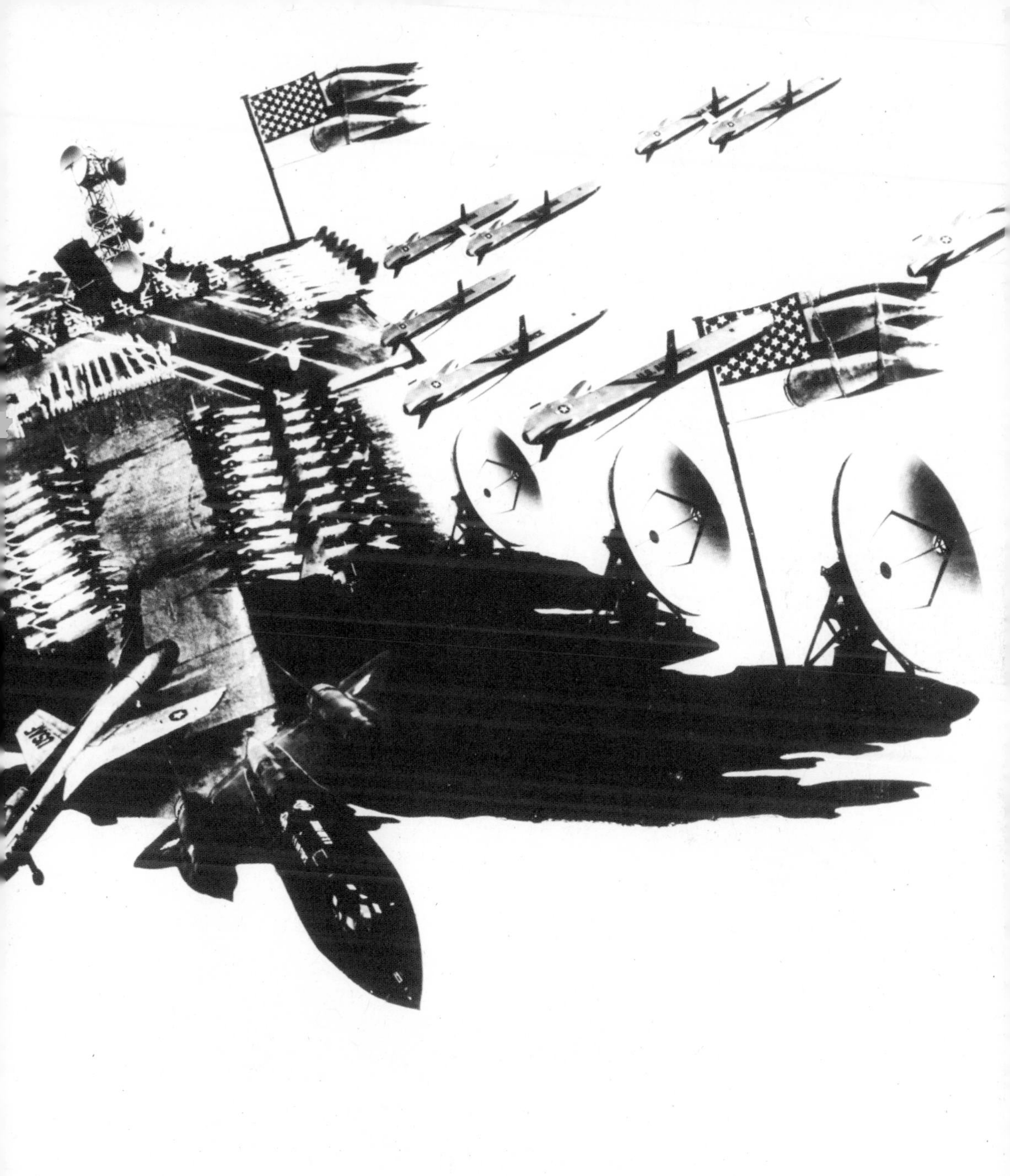

# 130000000000

The total cost of replacing the British Trident nuclear missile system is estimated at £130 billion

Greenpeace

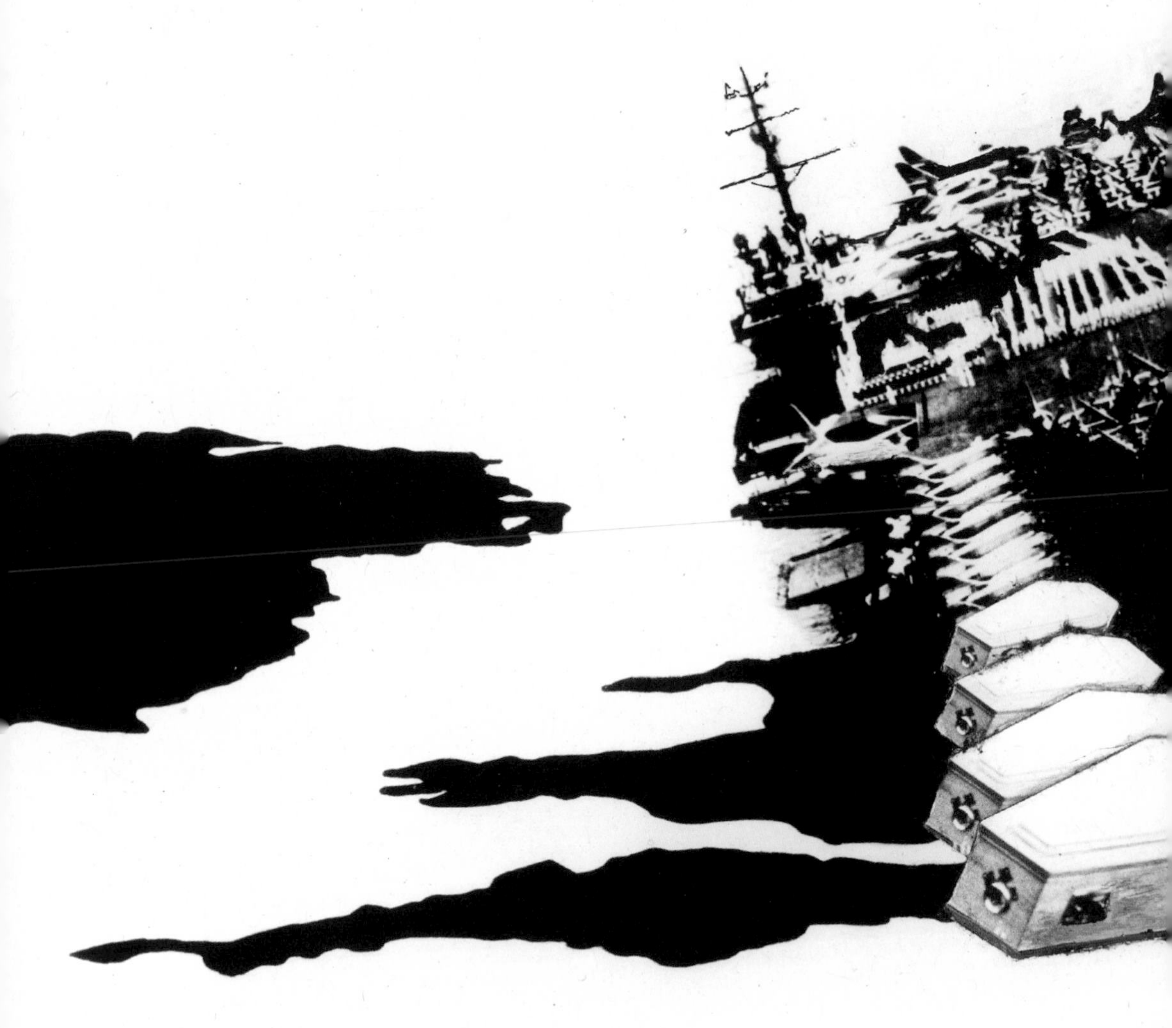

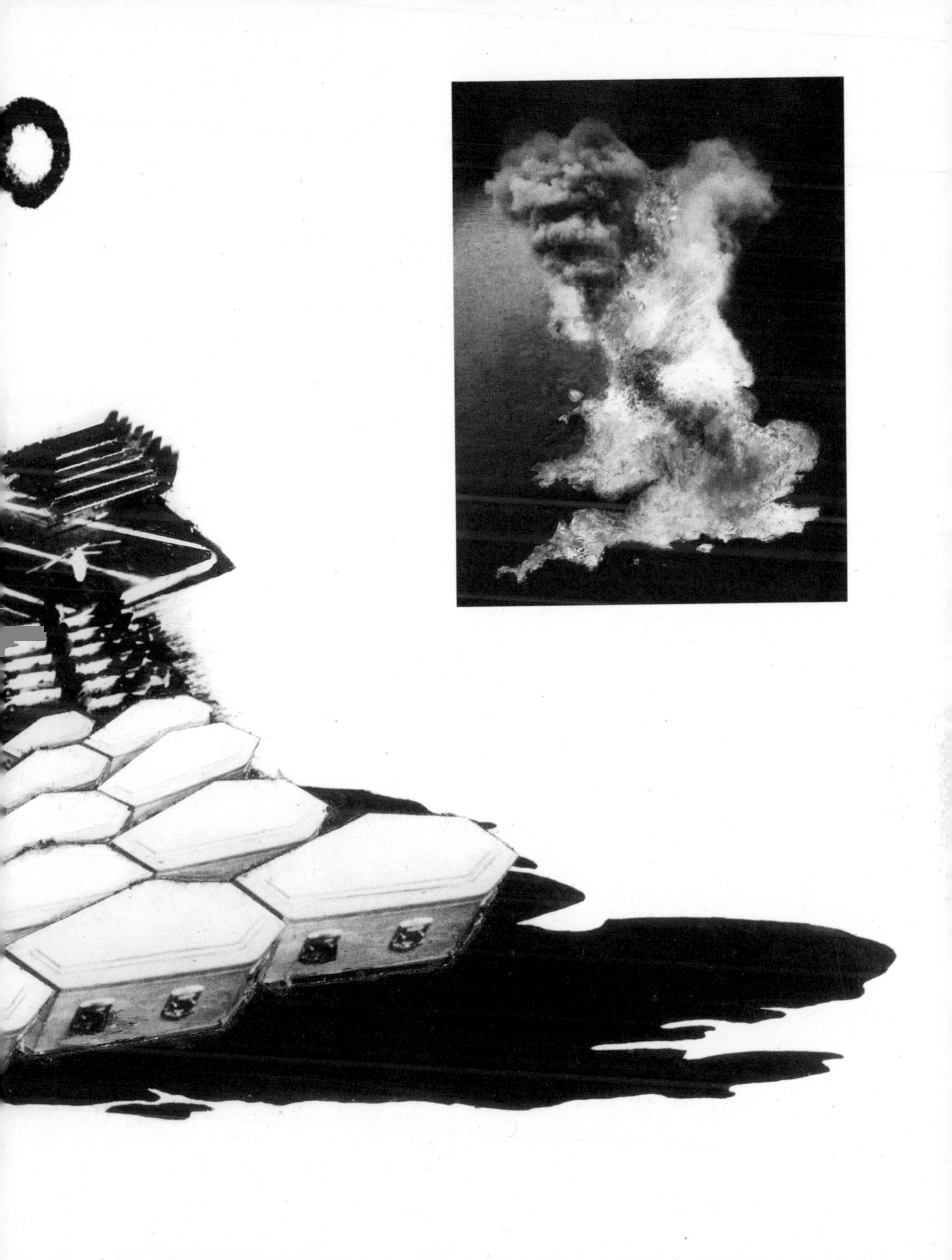

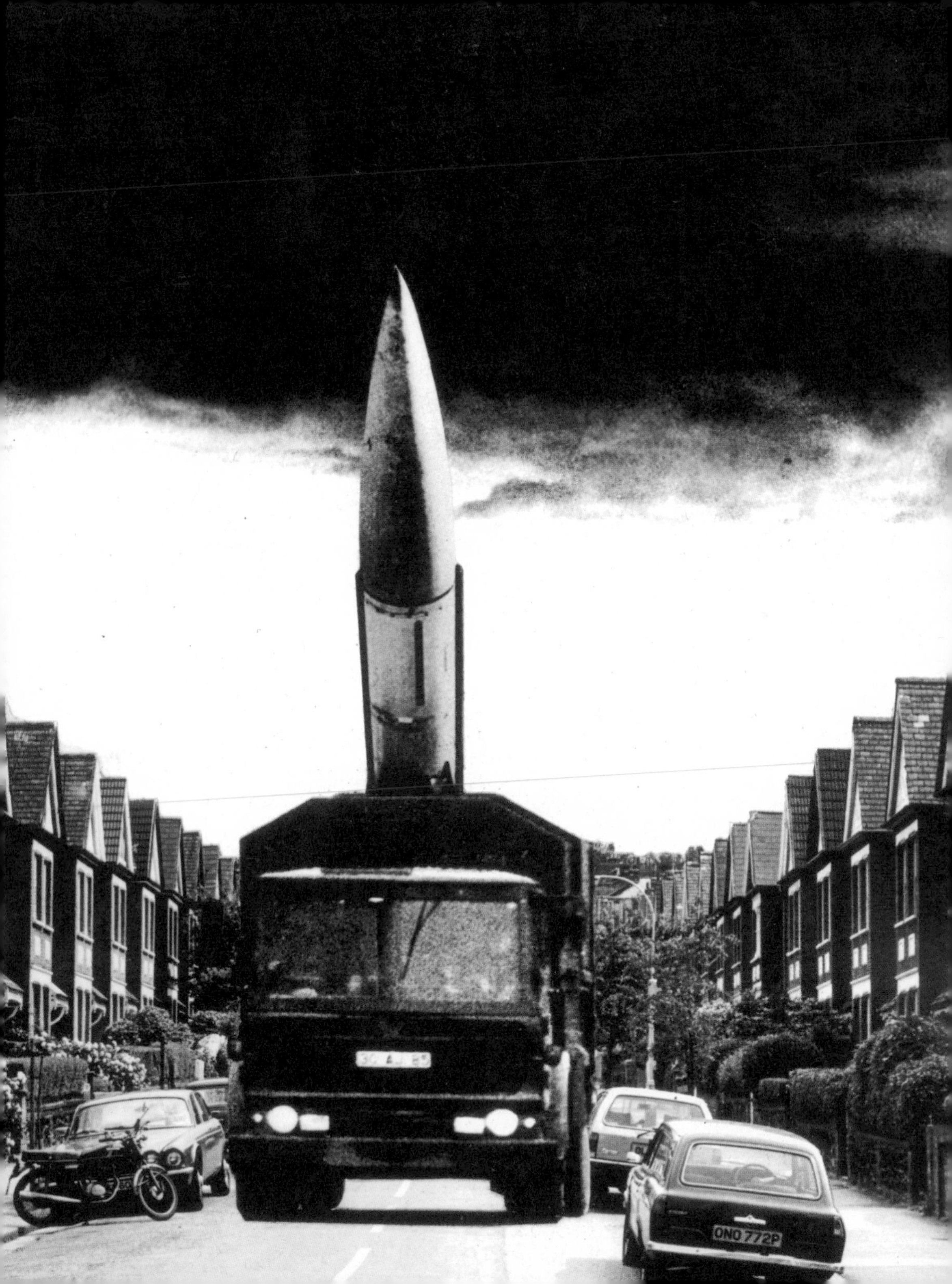
ONO 772P

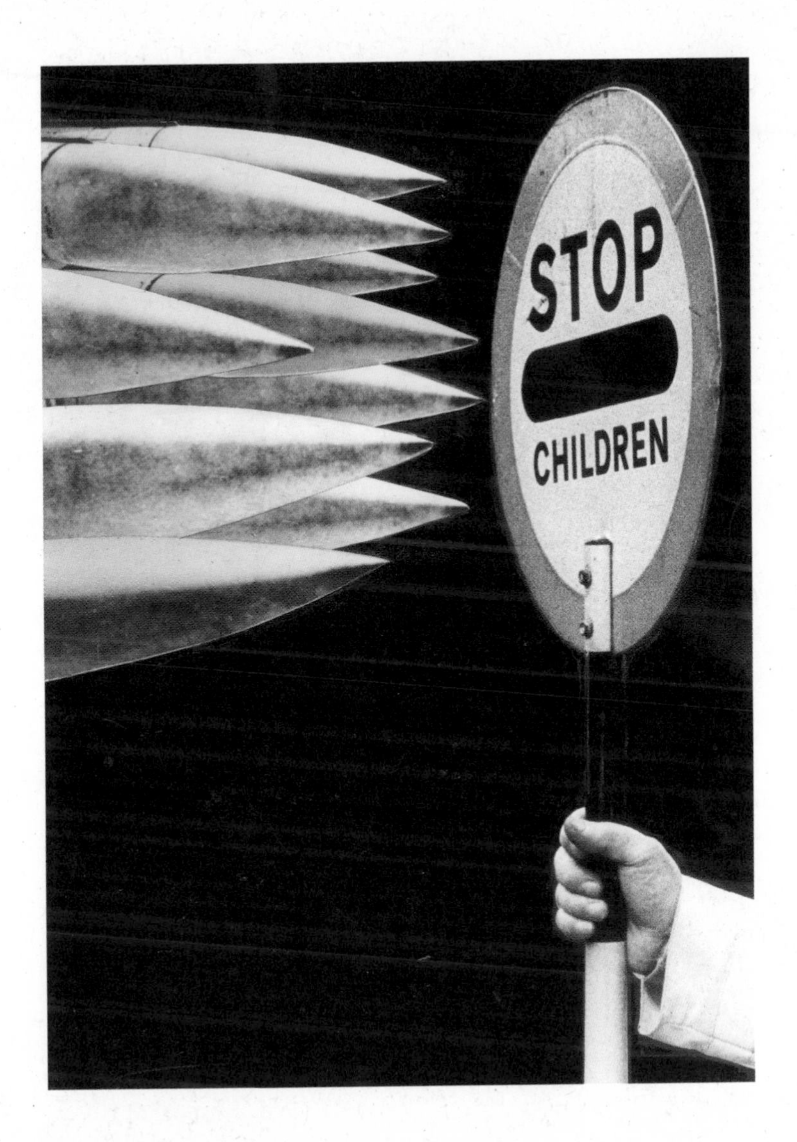


# 1900

Between 2001 and 2006 there were at least 1,900 military projects conducted in 26 UK universities, valued at approximately £275 million. The UK is the second biggest funder of military research and development in the world.

Joanna Bourke, *Wounding the World*

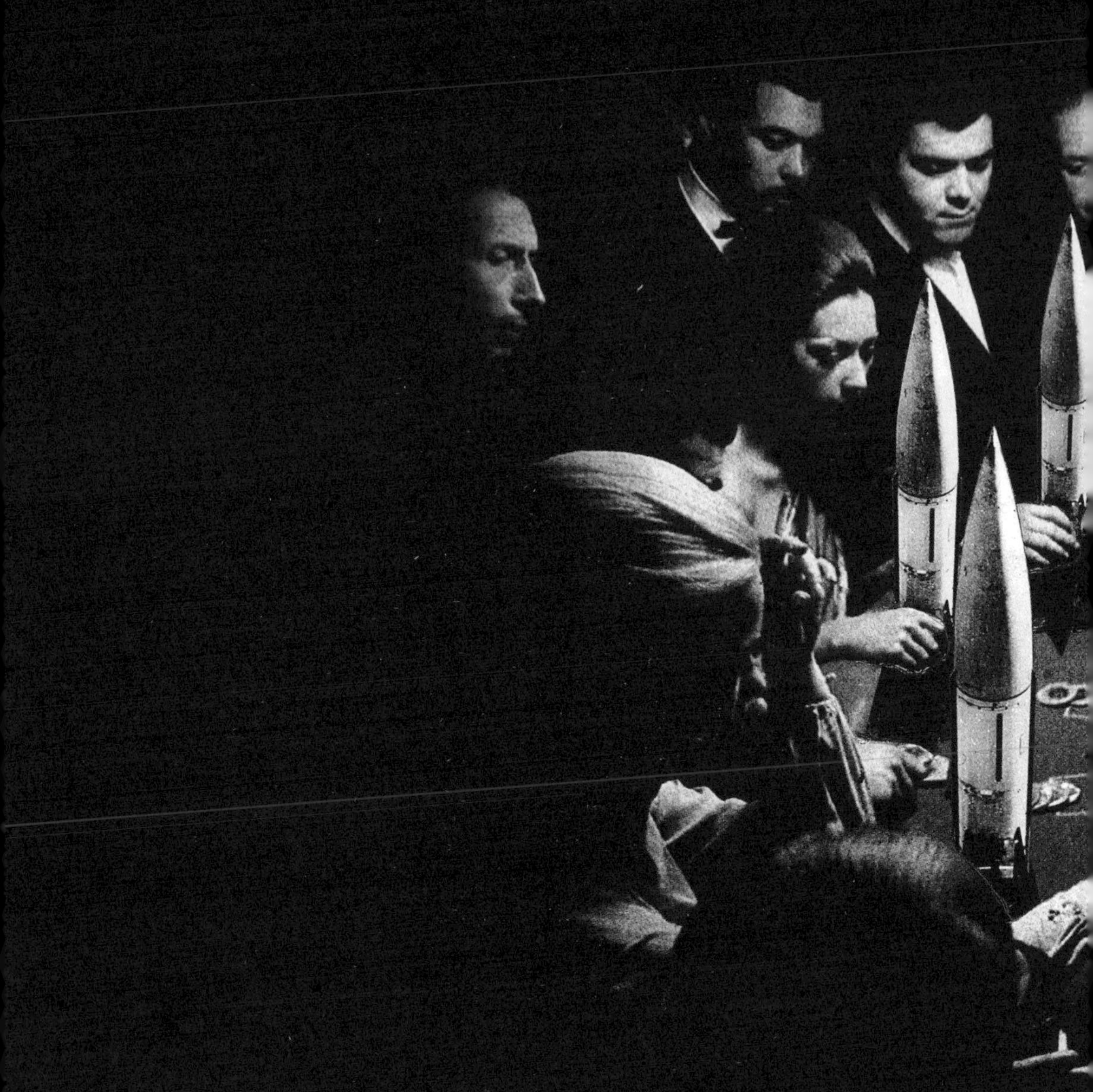

# 17270

The number of known nuclear weapons in the world in 2013 was 17,270

Stockholm International Peace Research Institute

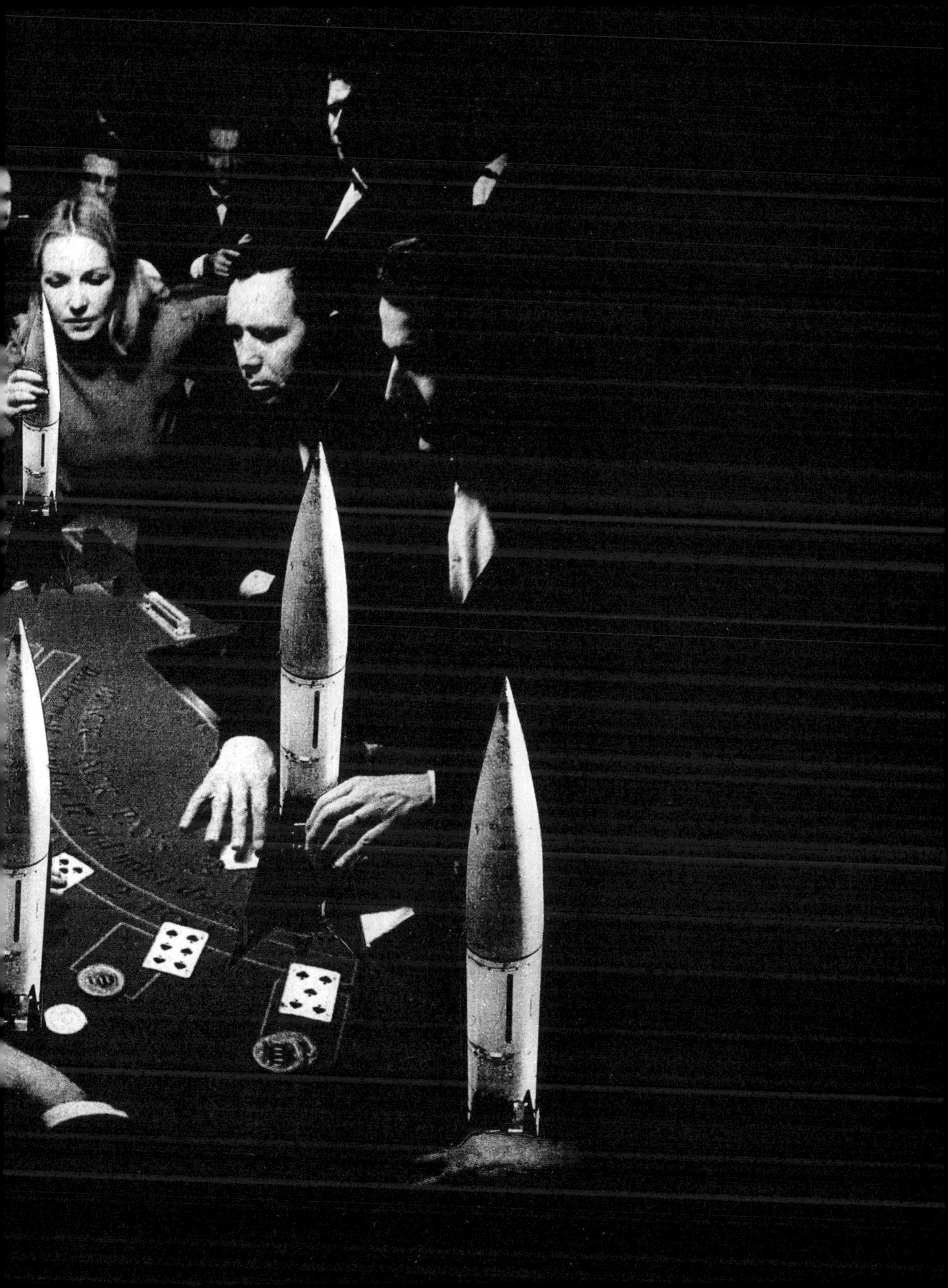

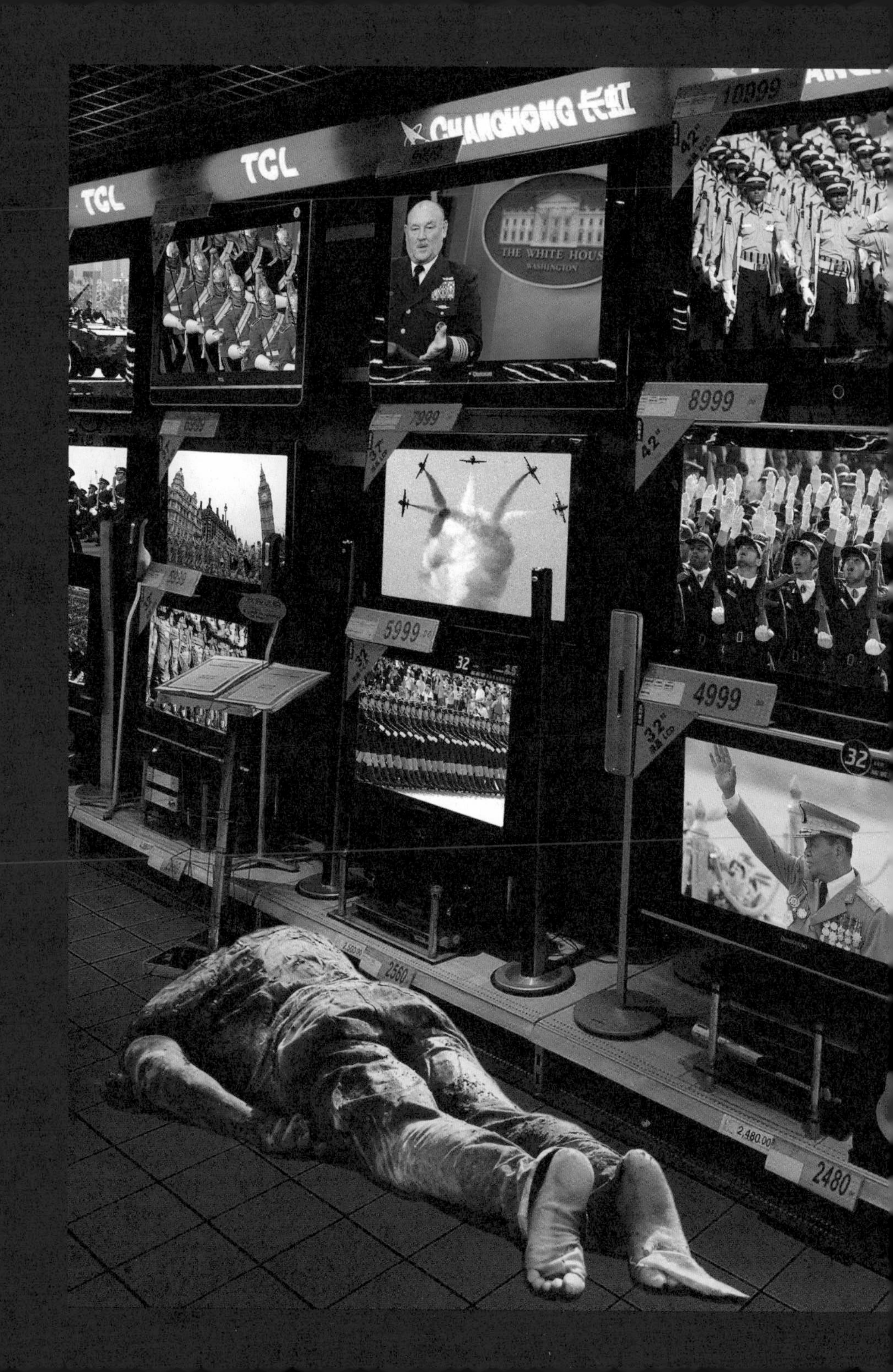

TCL
TCL
CHANGHONG 长虹
10999
THE WHITE HOUS
WASHINGTON
8999
7999
5999
4999
2560
2,480.00
2480

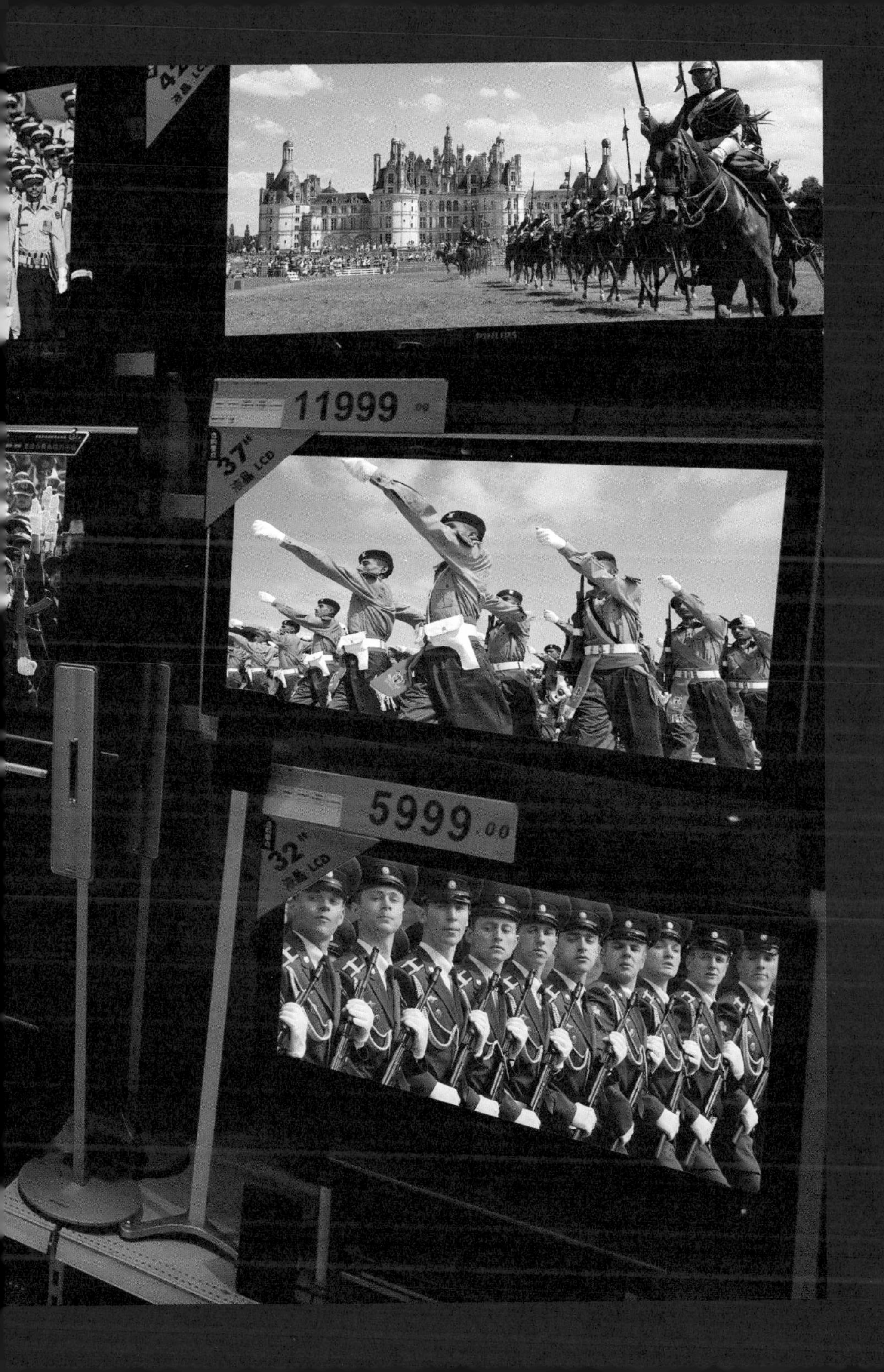
11999.00
37" 液晶 LCD
5999.00
32" 液晶 LCD

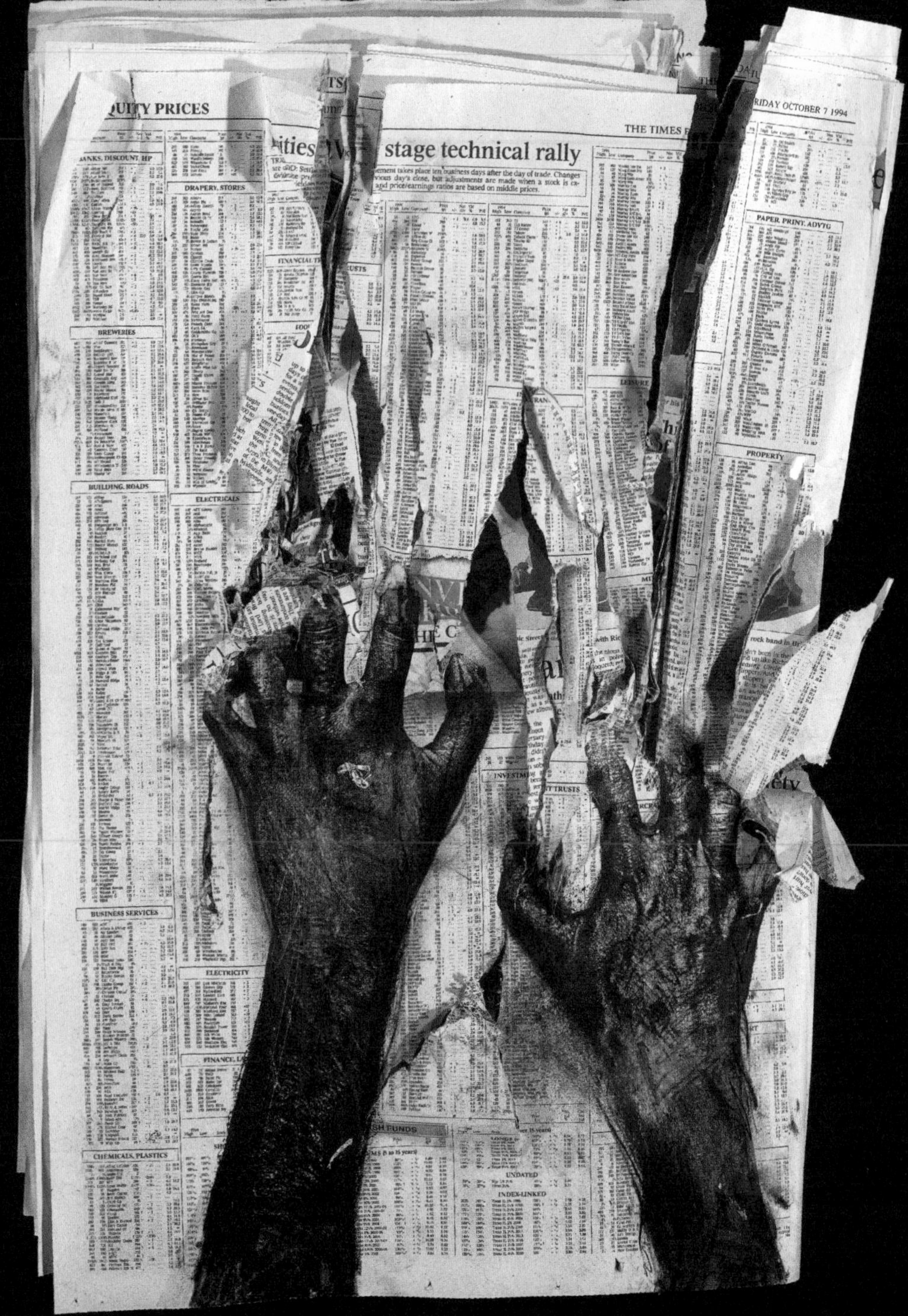
QUITY PRICES
THE TIMES
RIDAY OCTOBER 7 1994
stage technical rally
BANKS, DISCOUNT, HP
DRAPERY, STORES
BREWERIES
BUILDING, ROADS
ELECTRICALS
BUSINESS SERVICES
ELECTRICITY
CHEMICALS, PLASTICS
PAPER, PRINT, ADVTG
PROPERTY
UNDATED
INDEX-LINKED

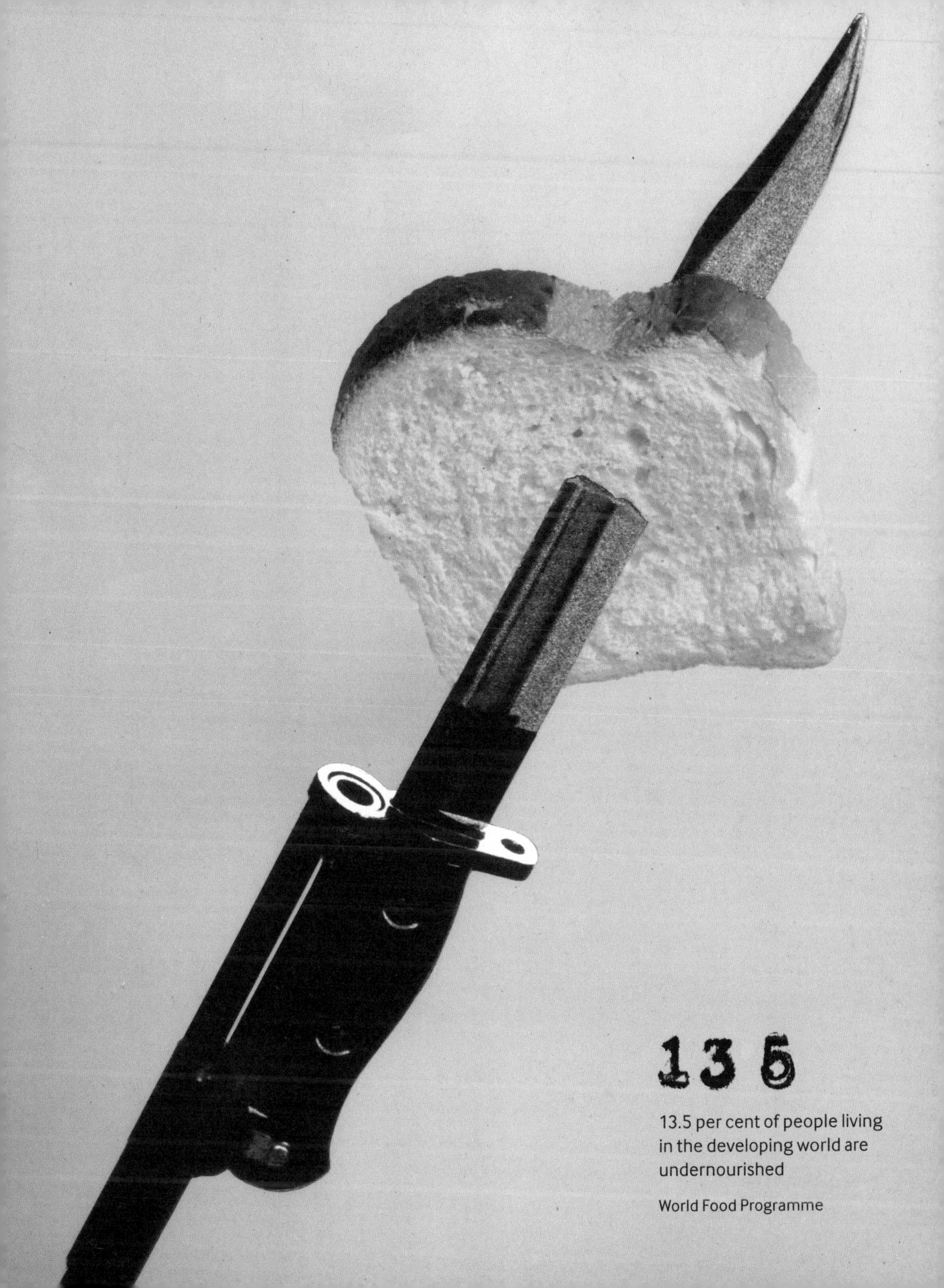
13 5
13.5 per cent of people living in the developing world are undernourished
World Food Programme

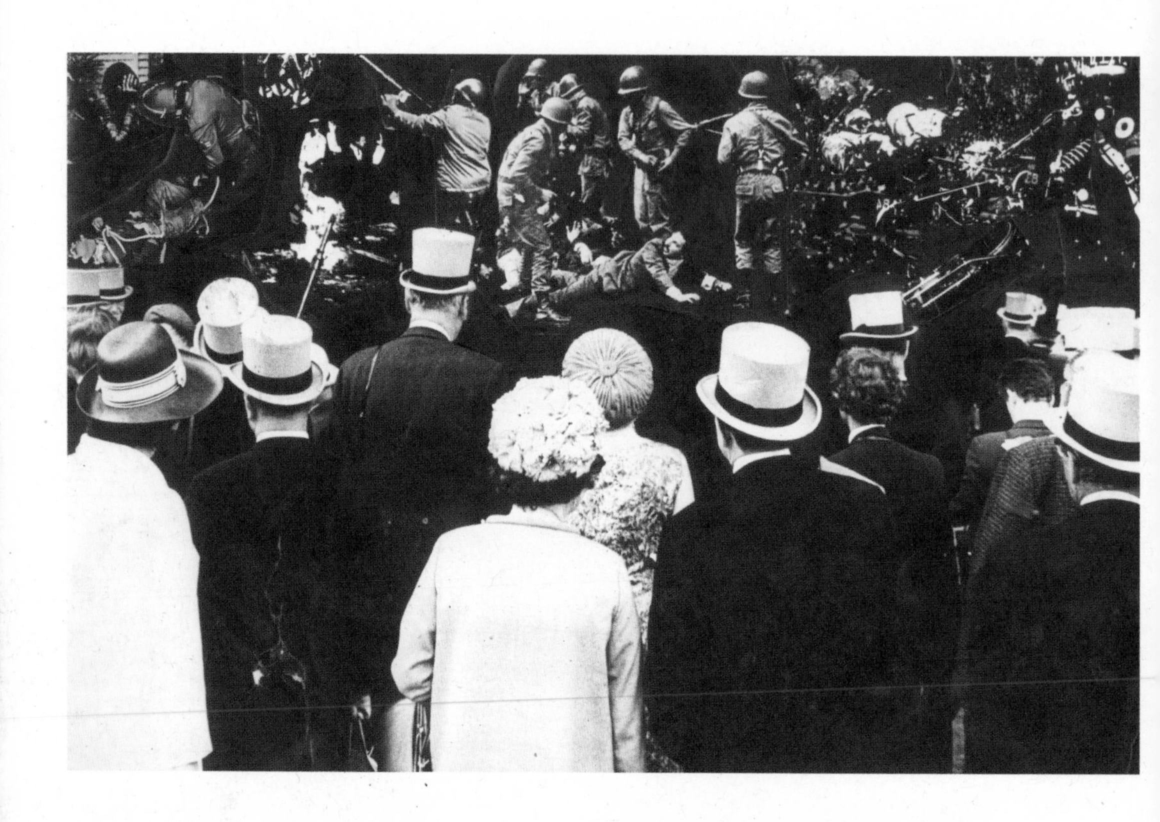

# 262000000

It is estimated that 262 million people were killed in the twentieth century by their own governments

Department of Political Science, University of Hawaii

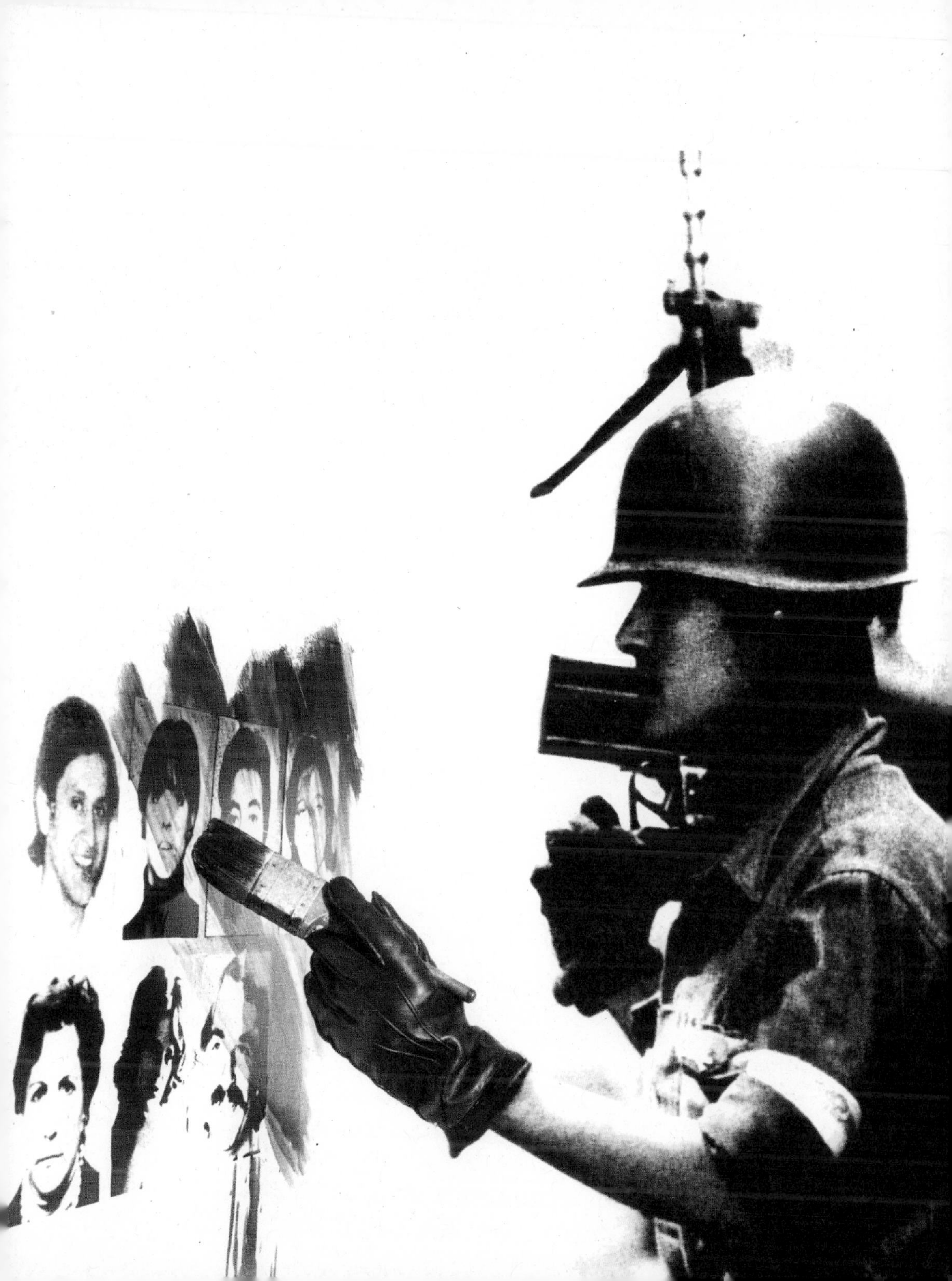

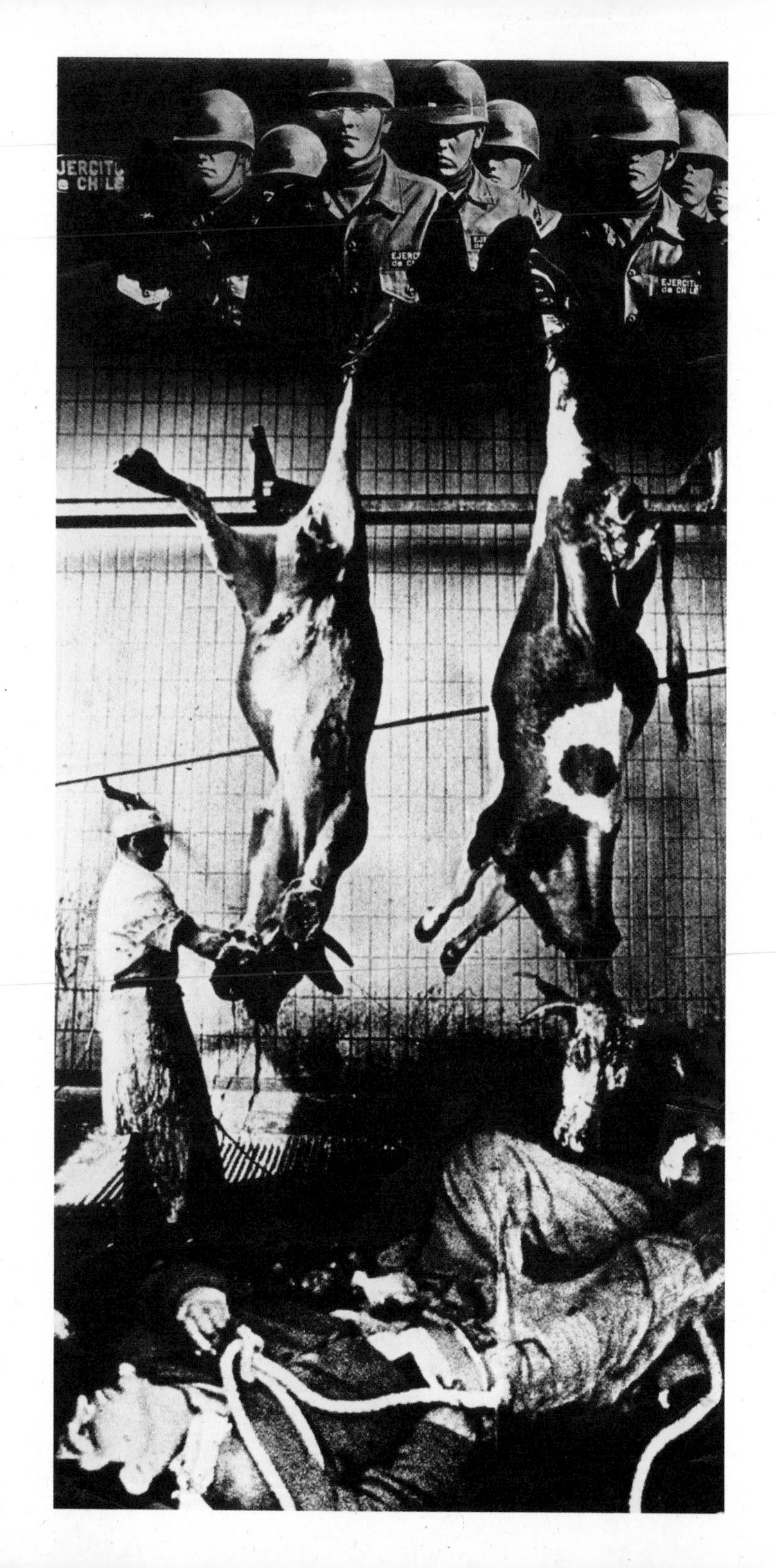
JERCIT
CHILE
EJERCIT
de CHILE

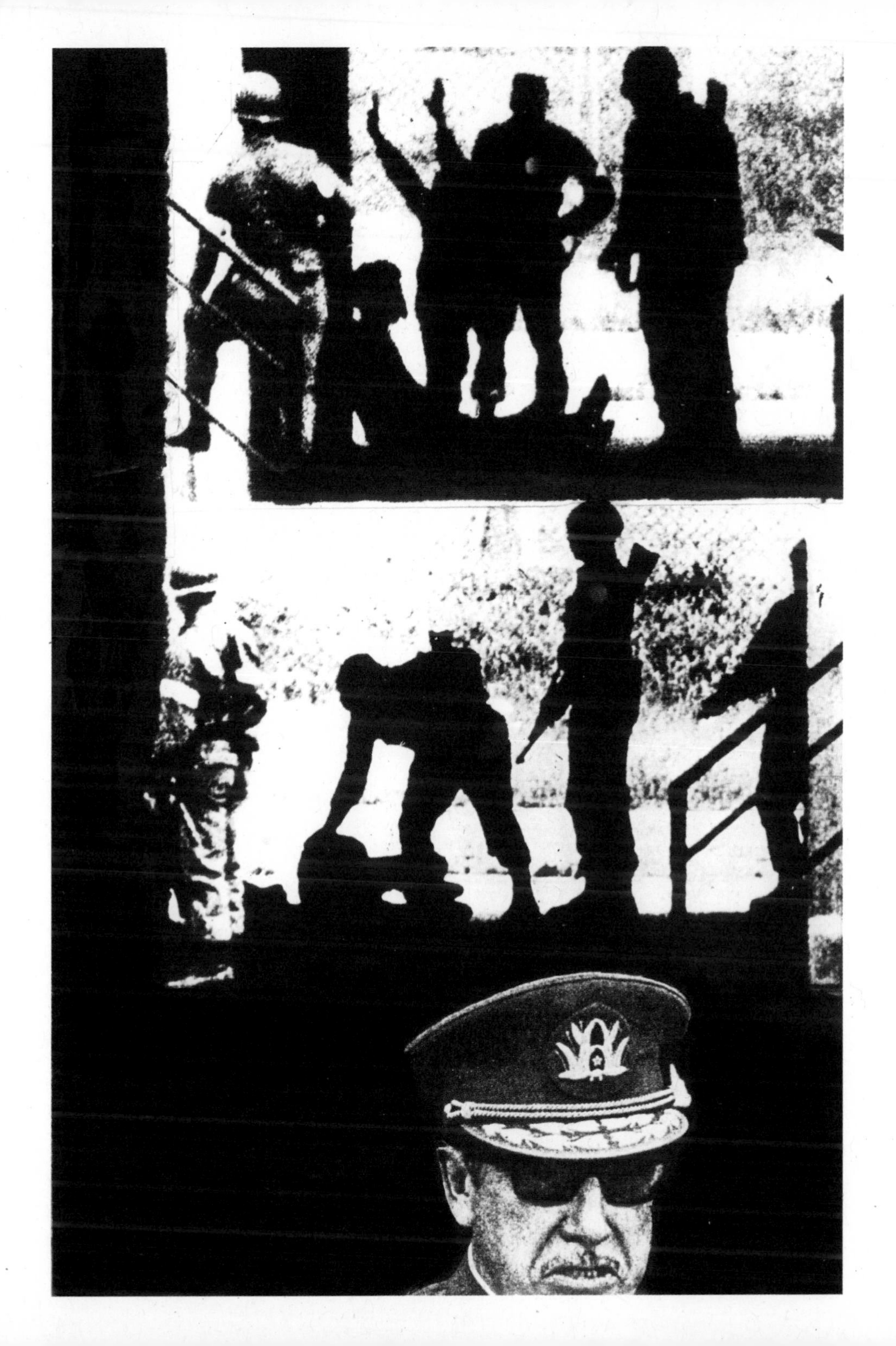

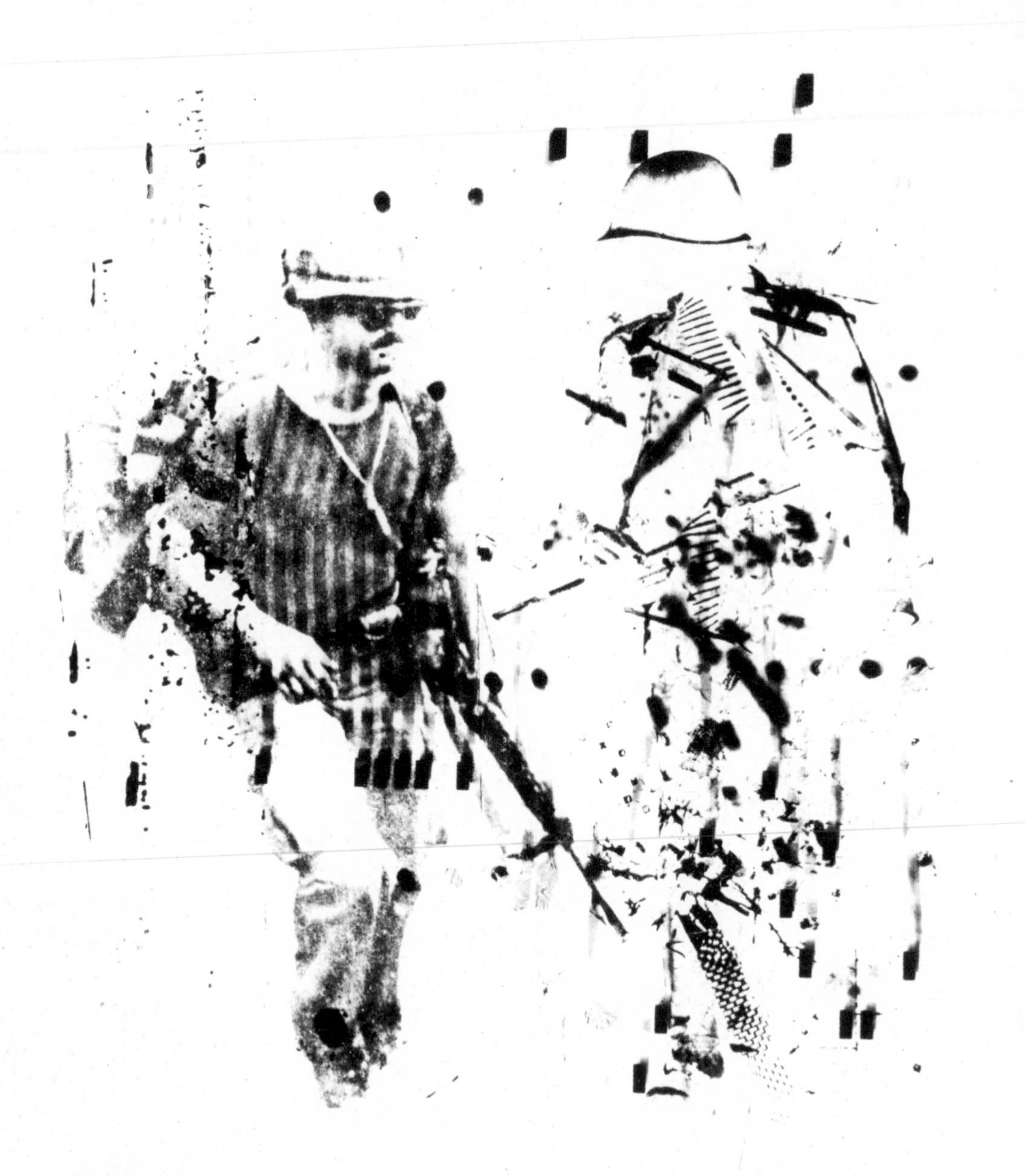

# 58148

58,148 Americans died in the Vietnam War

Armed Forces History Museum

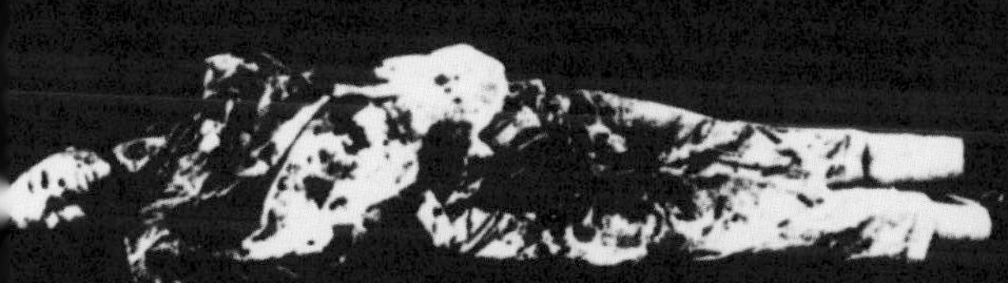

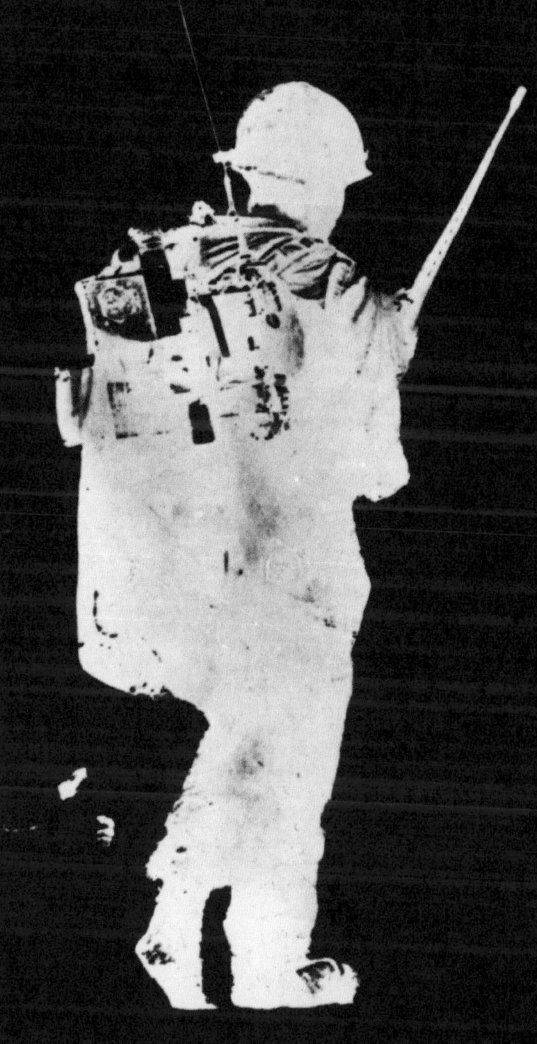

# 3800000

3.8 million Vietnamese died in the Vietnam War

British Medical Journal

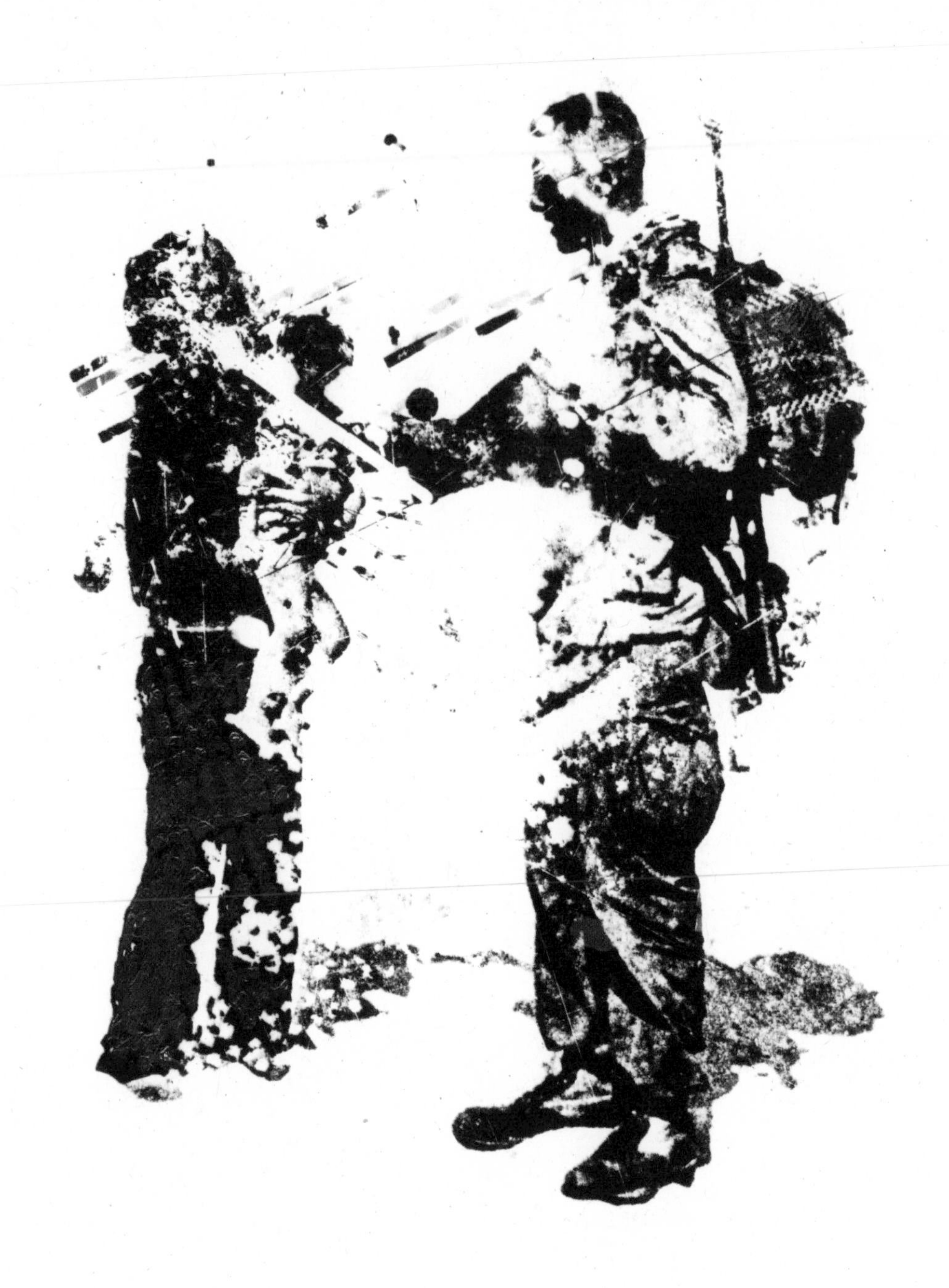

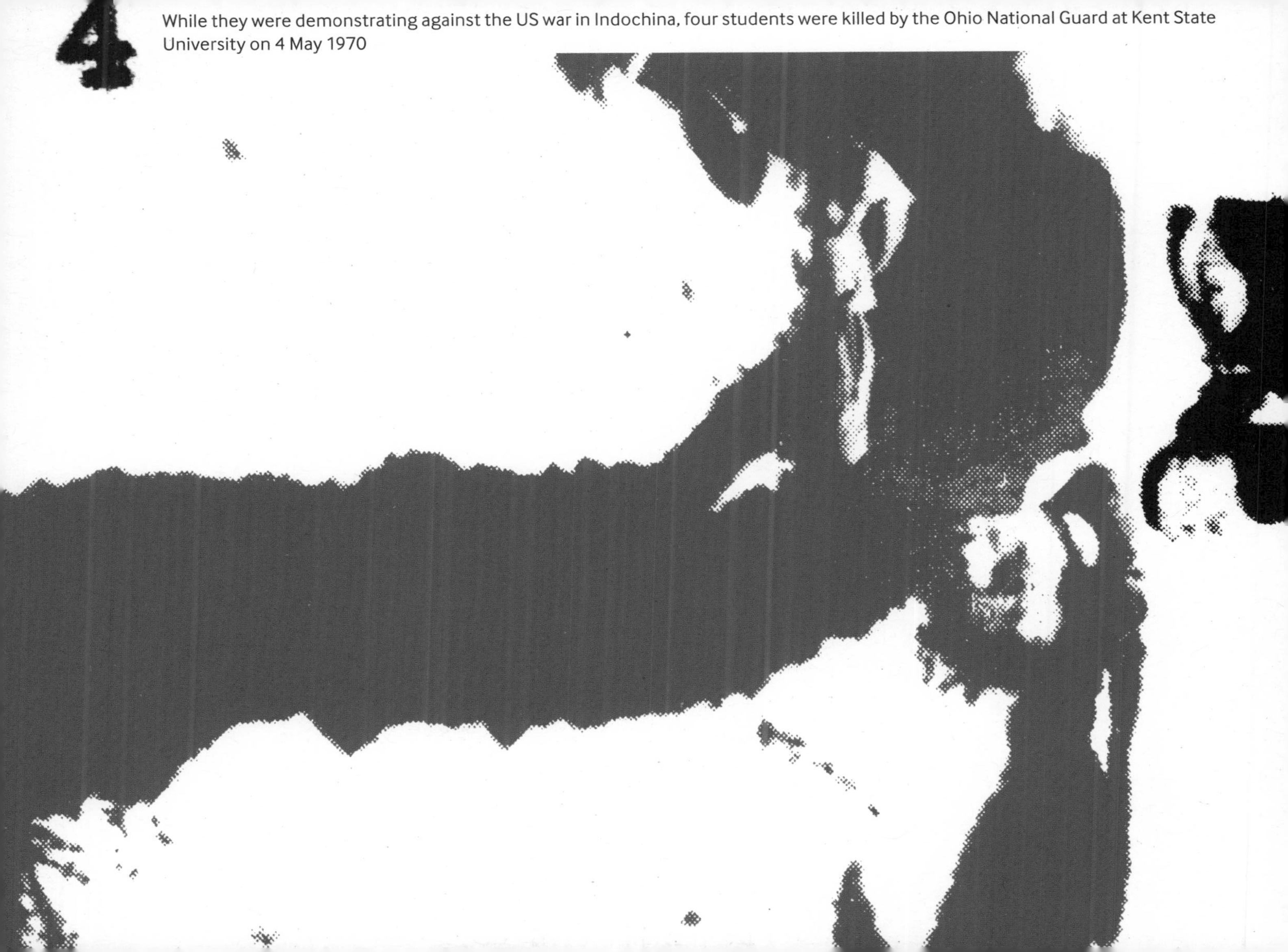

**4** While they were demonstrating against the US war in Indochina, four students were killed by the Ohio National Guard at Kent State University on 4 May 1970

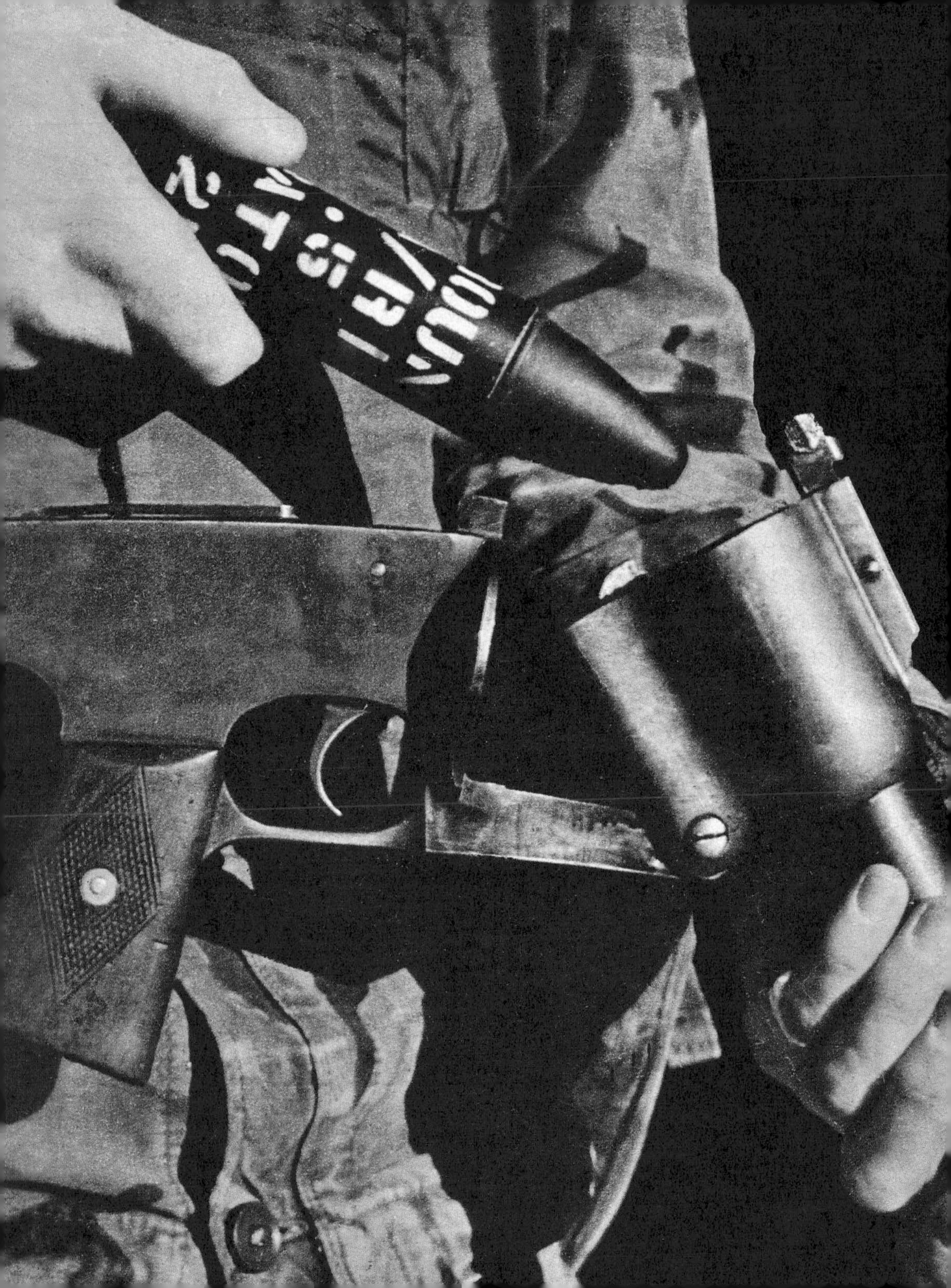

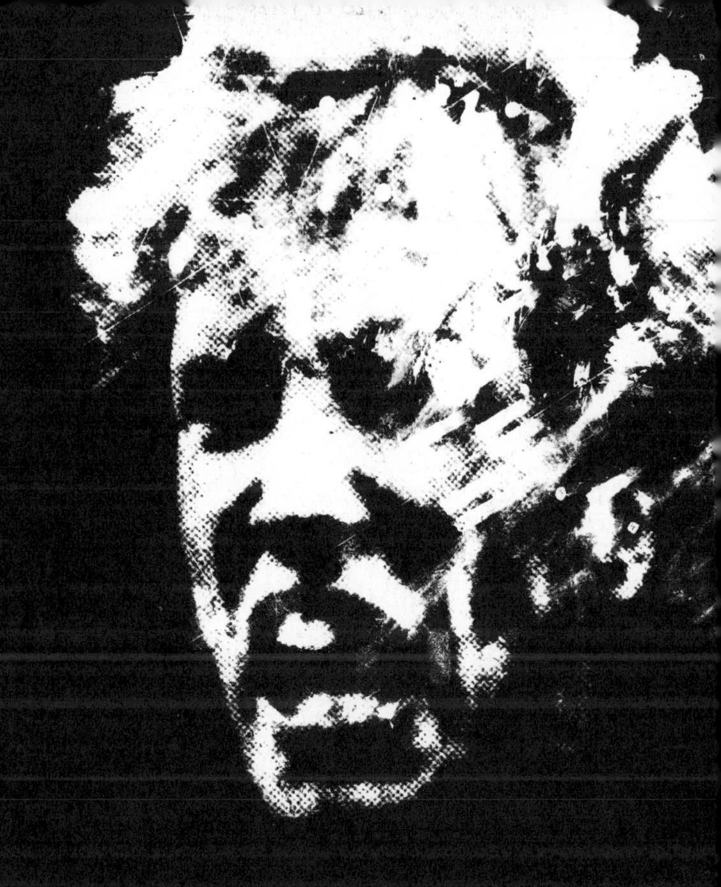

# 500000

An estimated half a million people are killed by firearms each year

United Nations Department of Disarmament Affairs

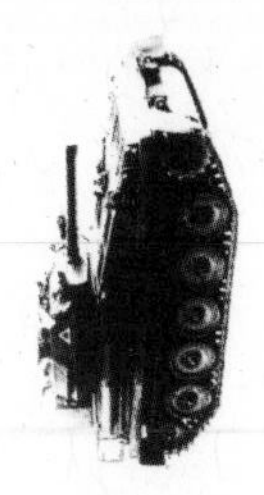
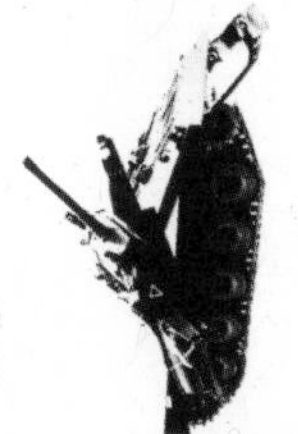
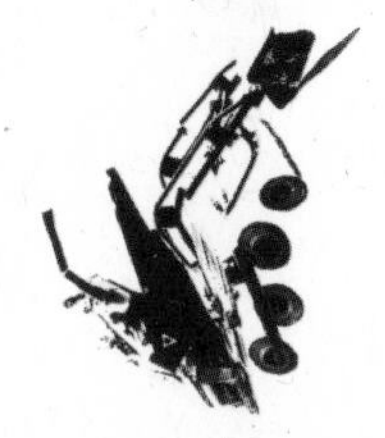
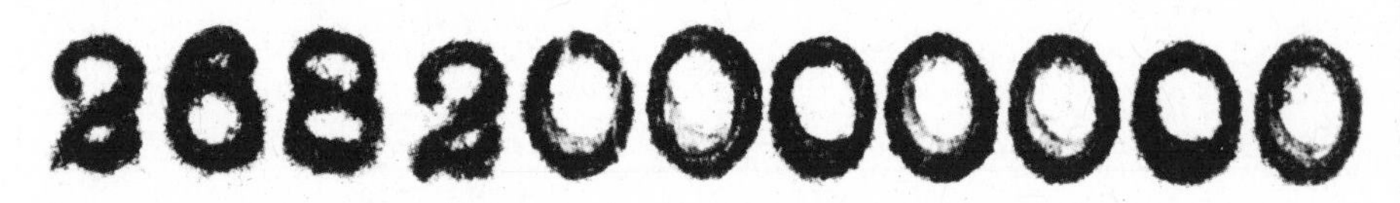


In 2013, British company BAE Systems' revenue was $26.82 billion

Stockholm International Peace Research Institute

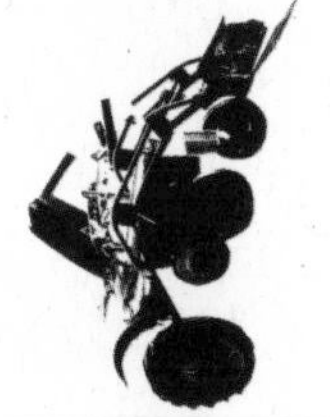
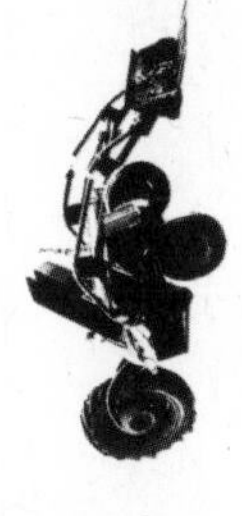
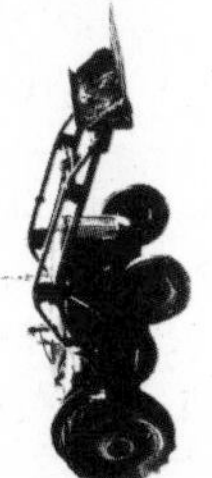

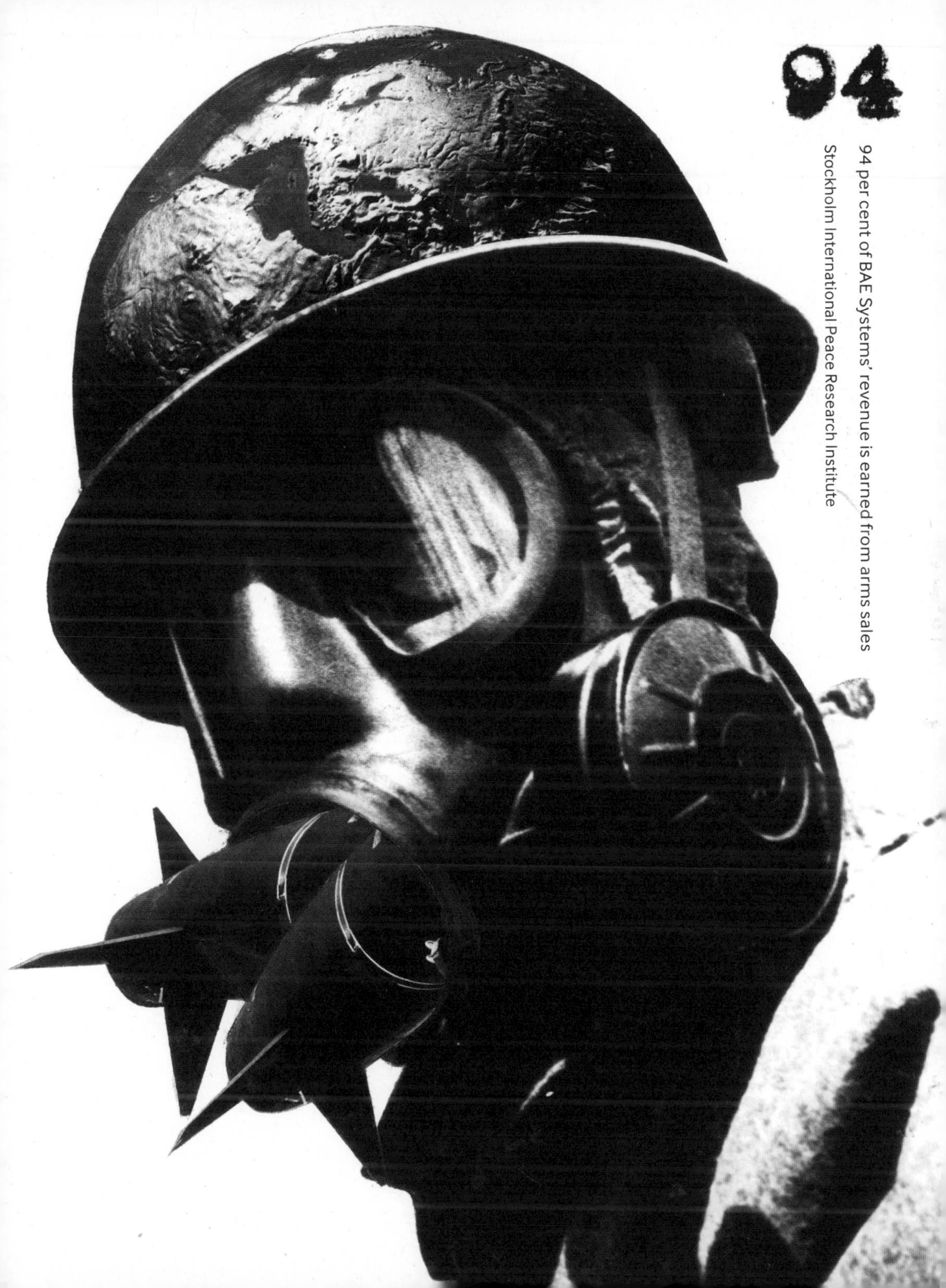
94
94 per cent of BAE Systems' revenue is earned from arms sales
Stockholm International Peace Research Institute

# 150

The number of countries that supported a 2014 UN General Assembly resolution recognising the need for international assistance for countries affected by depleted uranium contamination

United Nations General Assembly vote, 2014

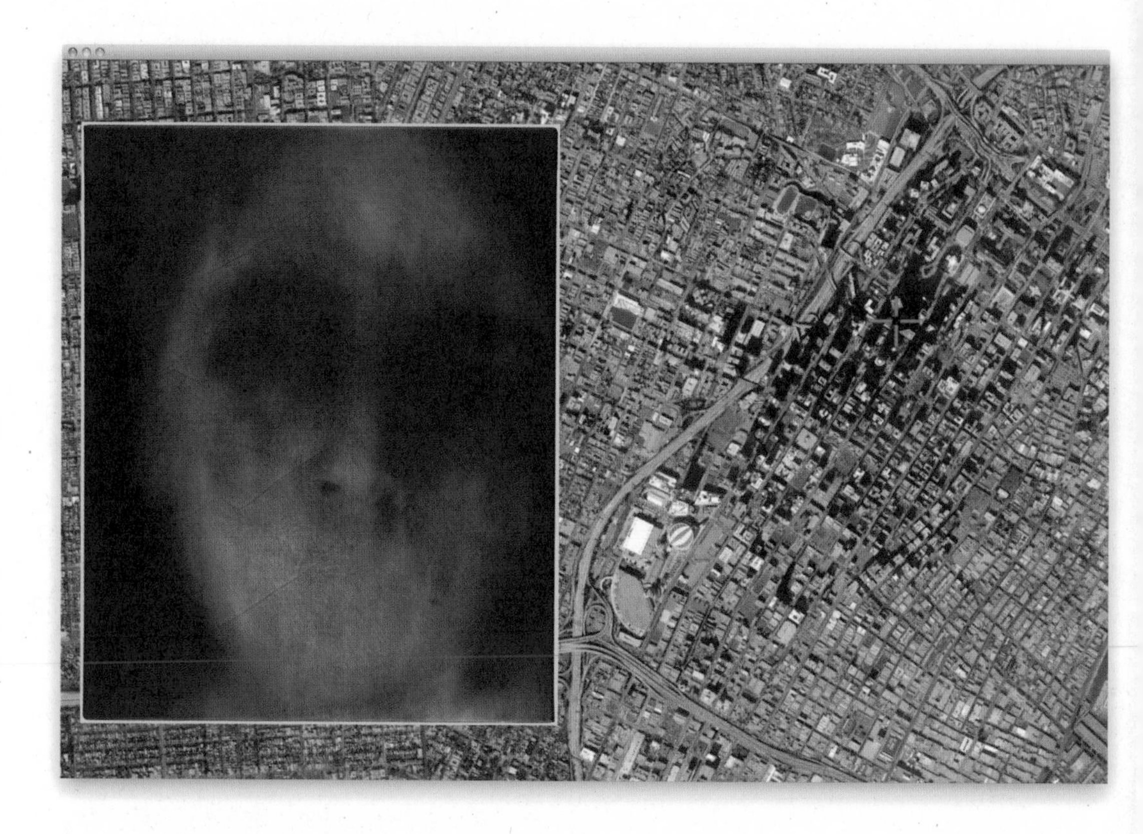

# 4

The number of countries that opposed the depleted uranium resolution. These were the UK, US, France and Israel. Depleted uranium is both chemically and radiologically toxic, the most affected organs being the kidneys and lungs.

United Nations General Assembly vote, 2014

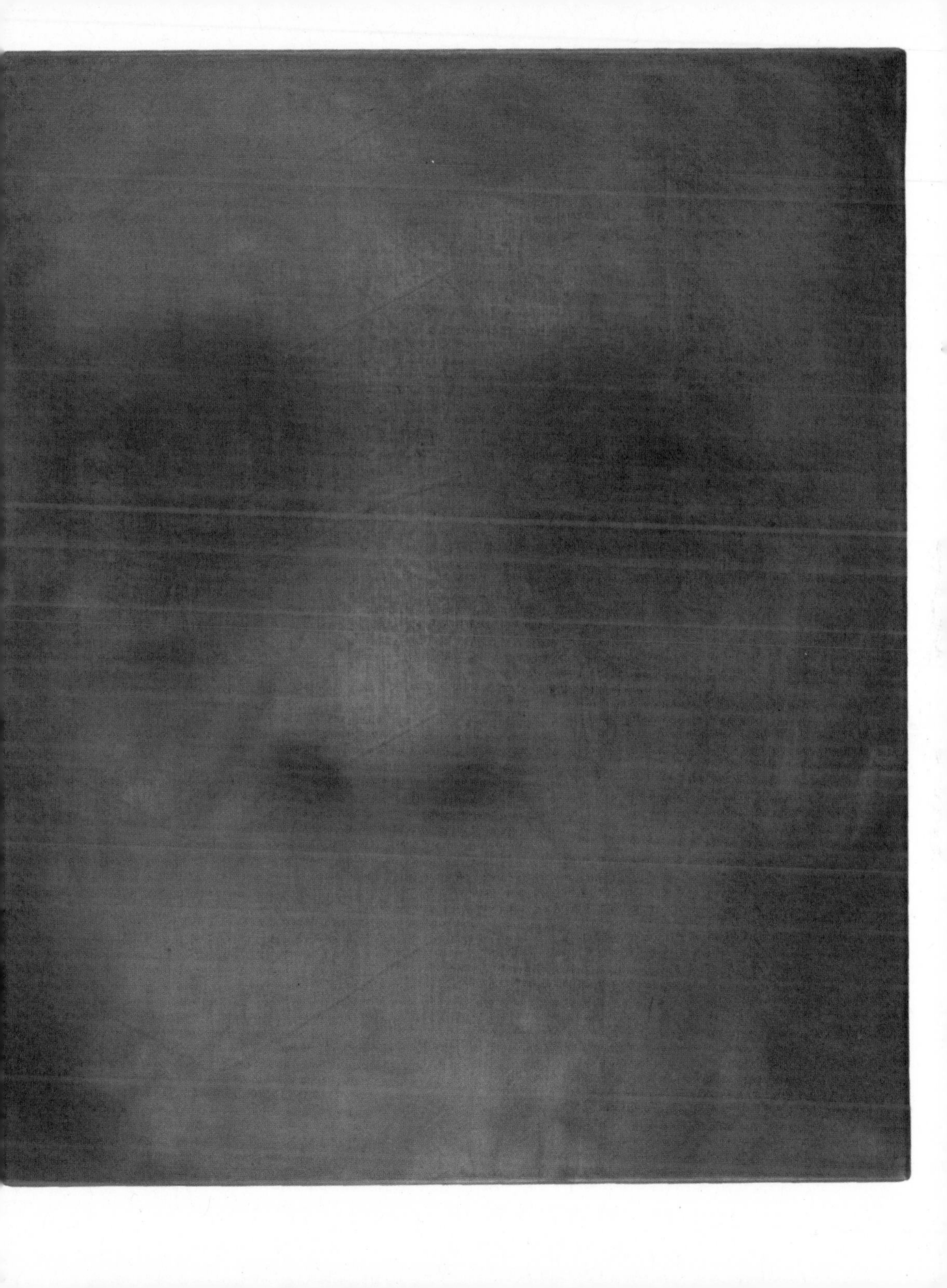

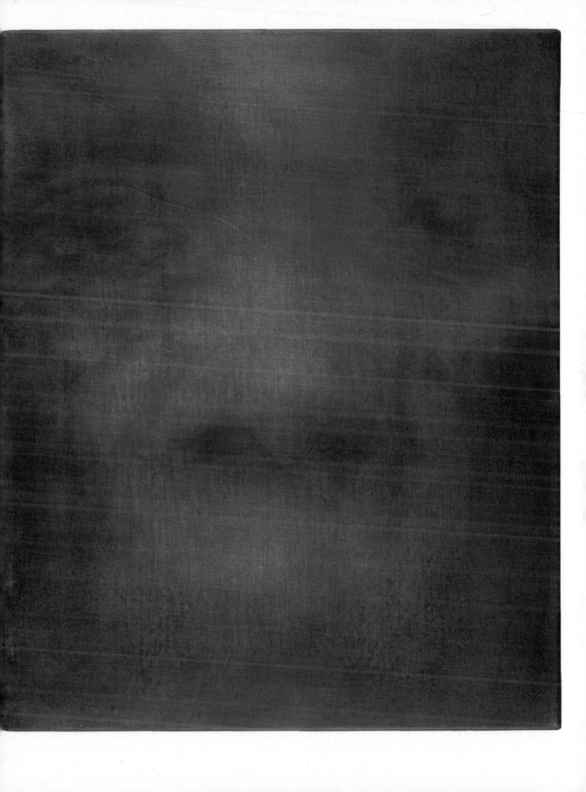

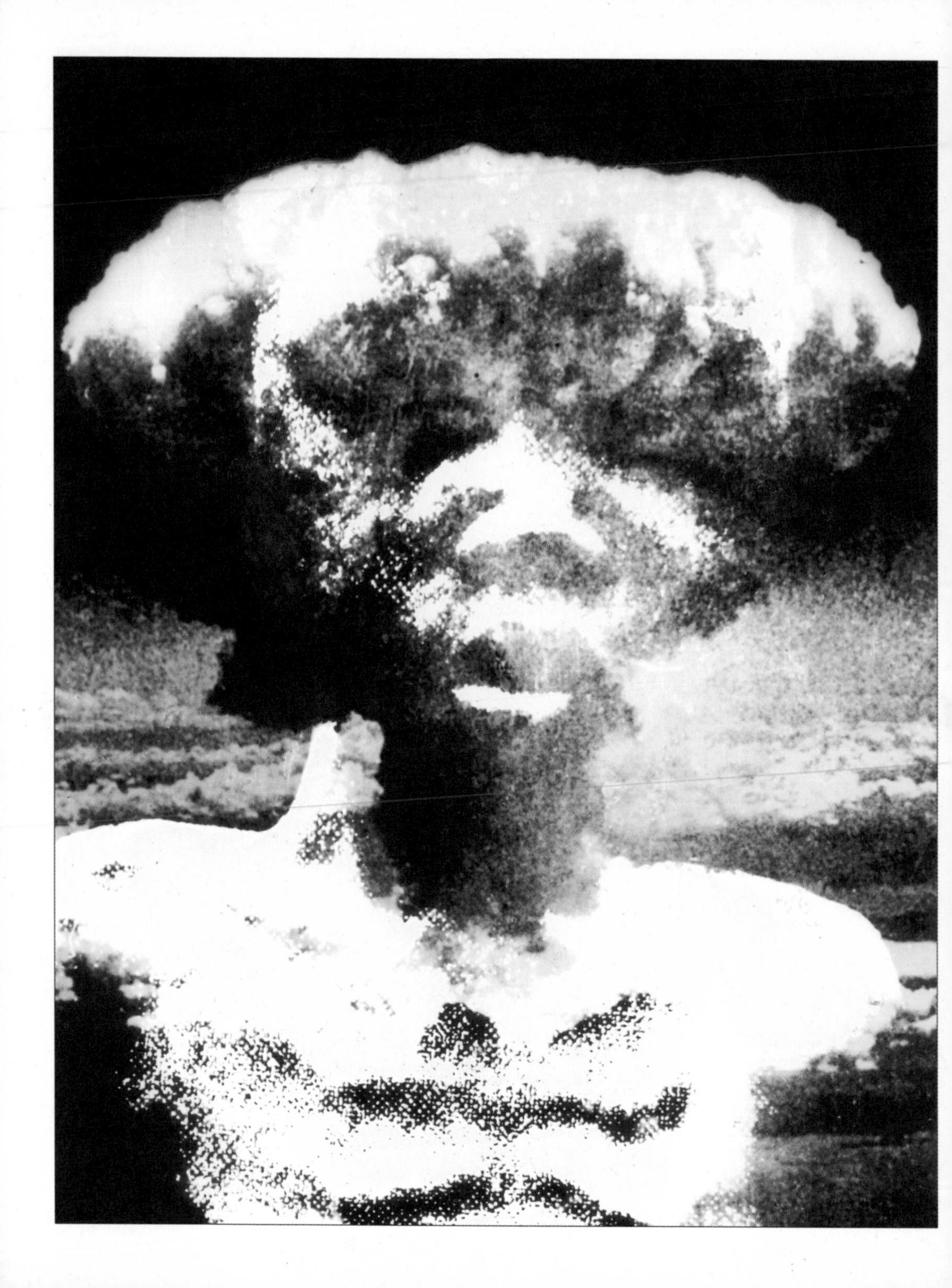

# 402000000000

In 2013, the top 100 arms-producing and military service companies (excluding China, for which no information is available) sold $402 billion worth of military hardware

Stockholm International Peace Research Institute

**37000000**

37 million land mines are still buried throughout Africa

Mines Advisory Group

The number of people who die or who are seriously injured by land mines each day

Mines Advisory Group

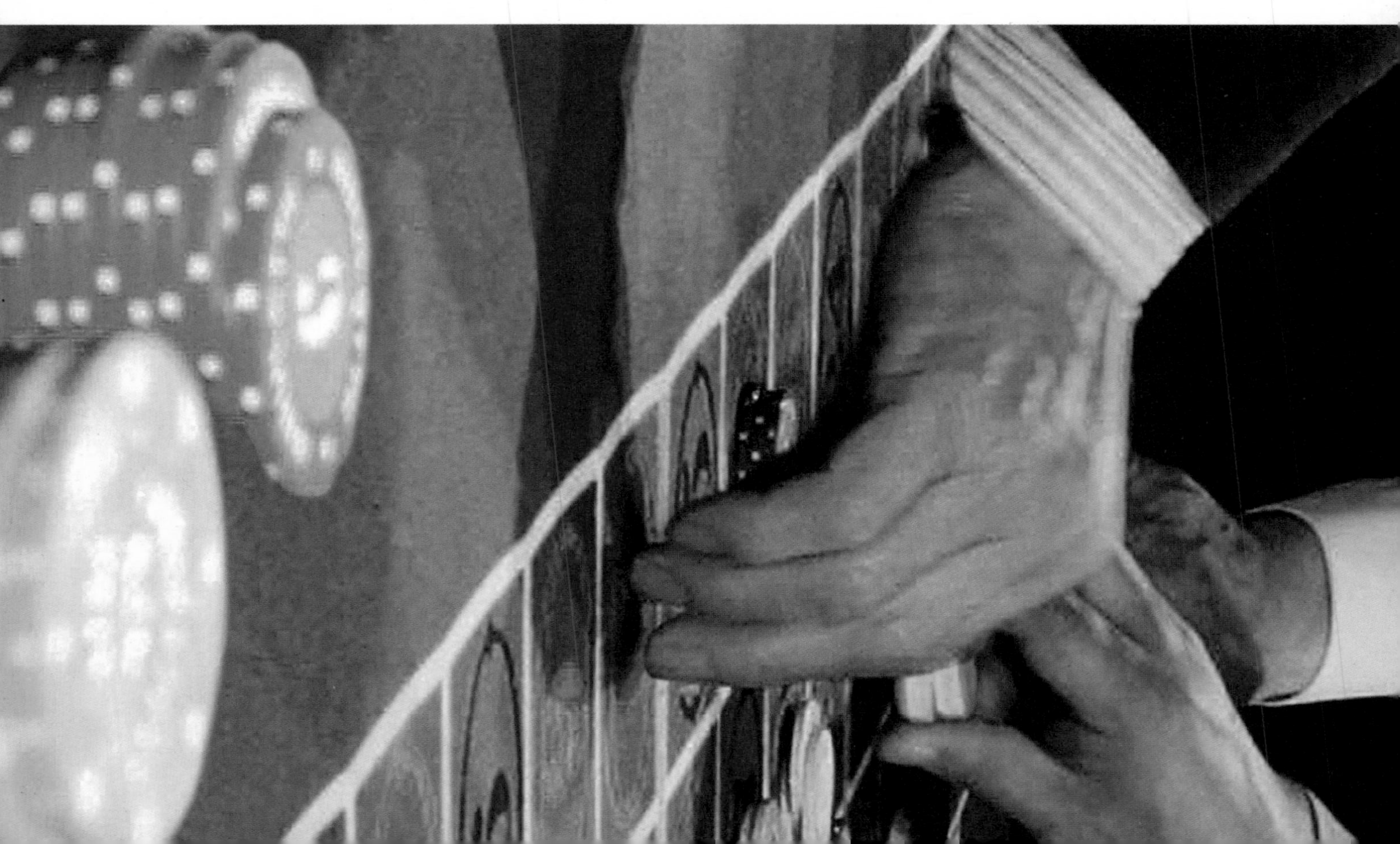

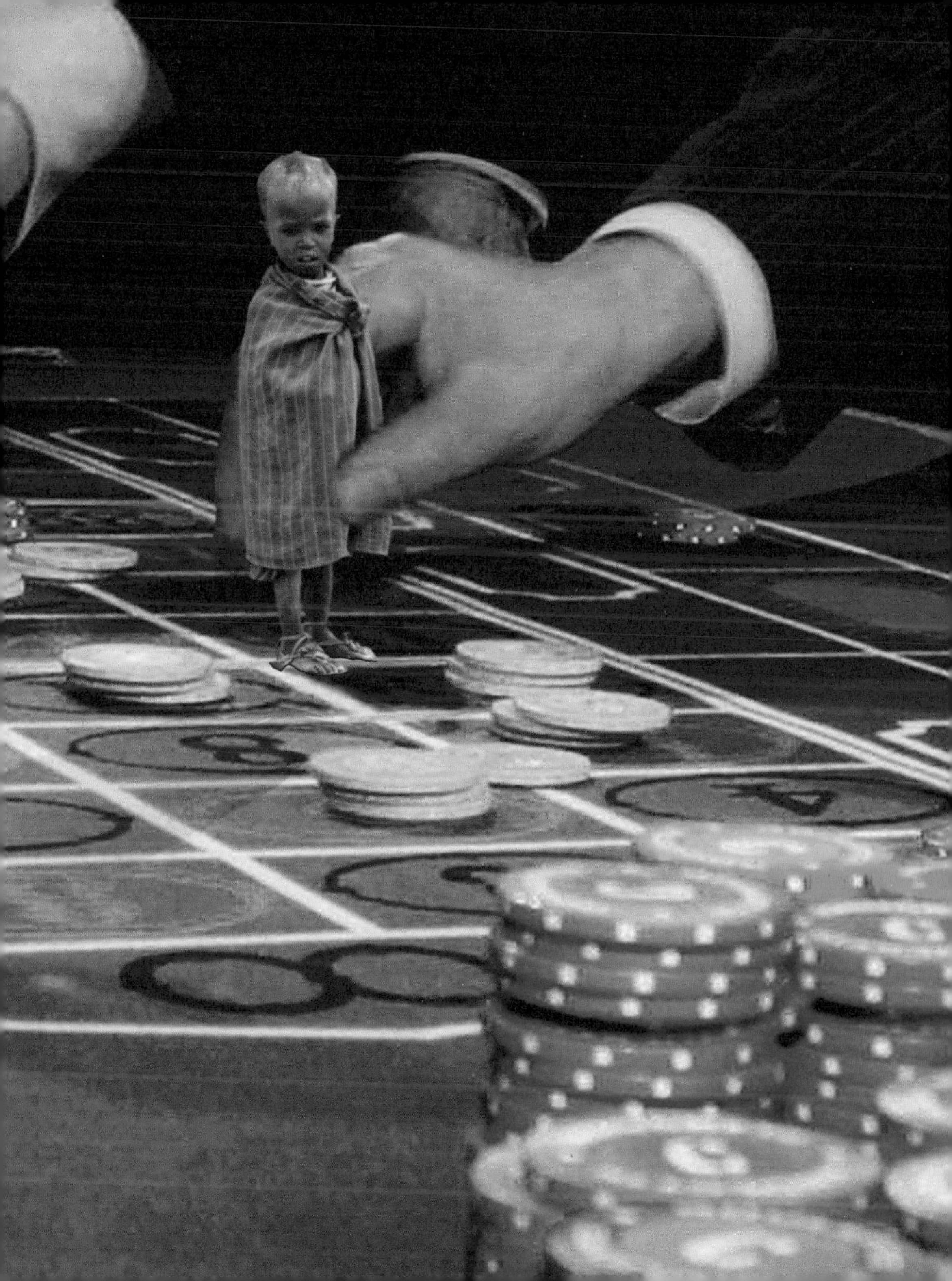

805000000

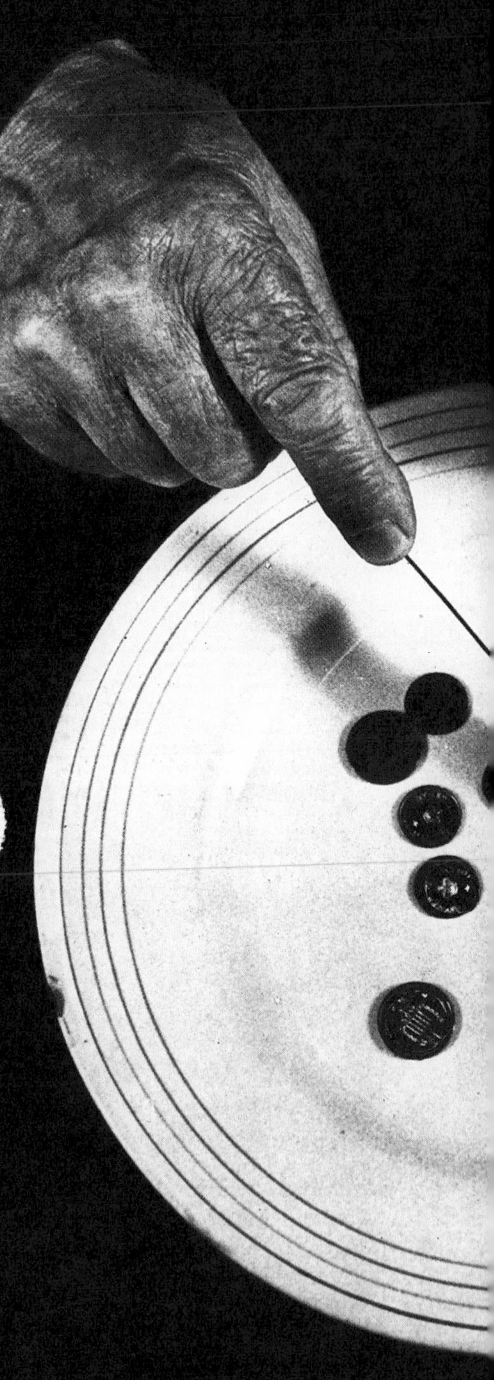

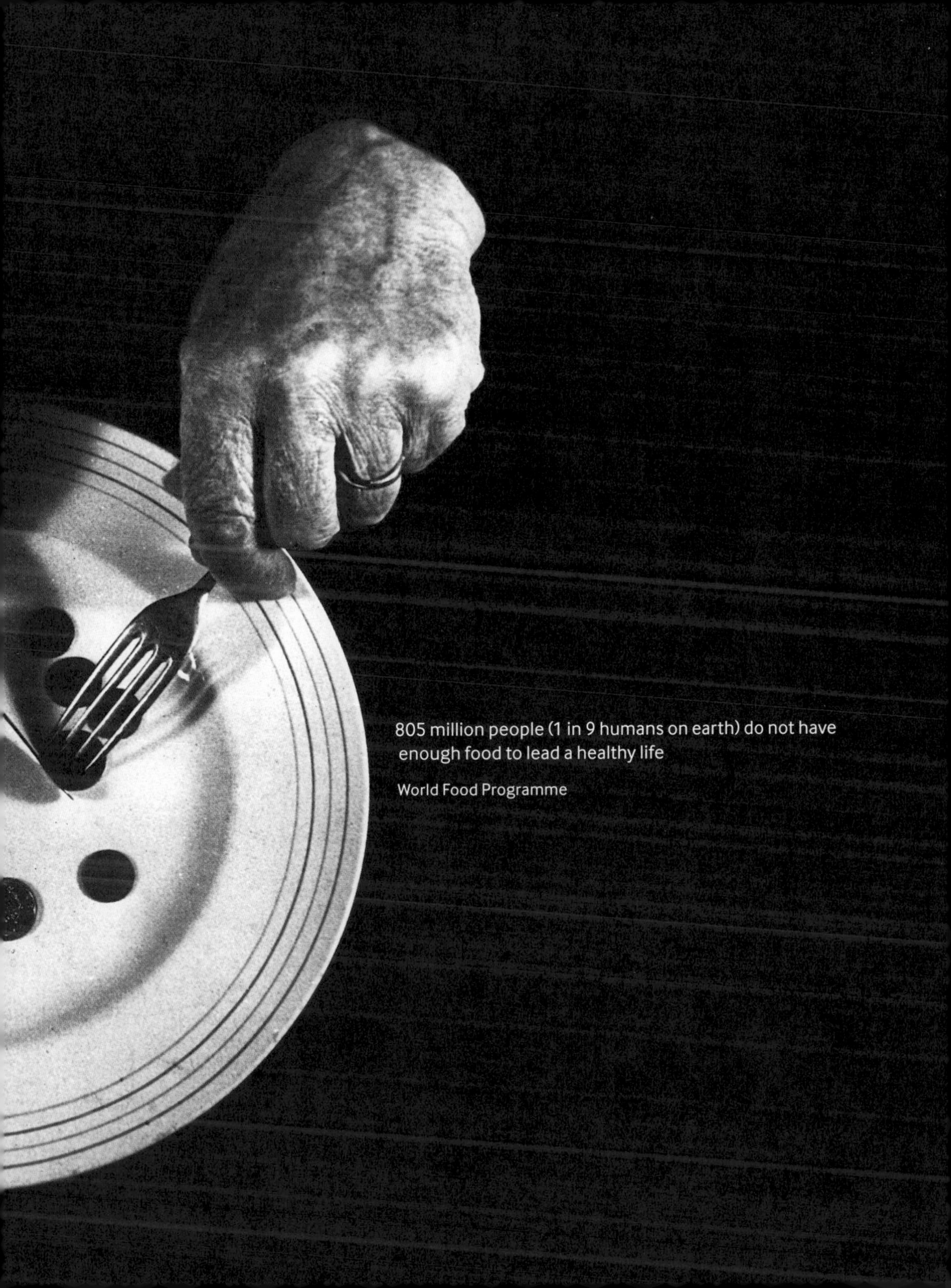
805 million people (1 in 9 humans on earth) do not have
enough food to lead a healthy life
World Food Programme

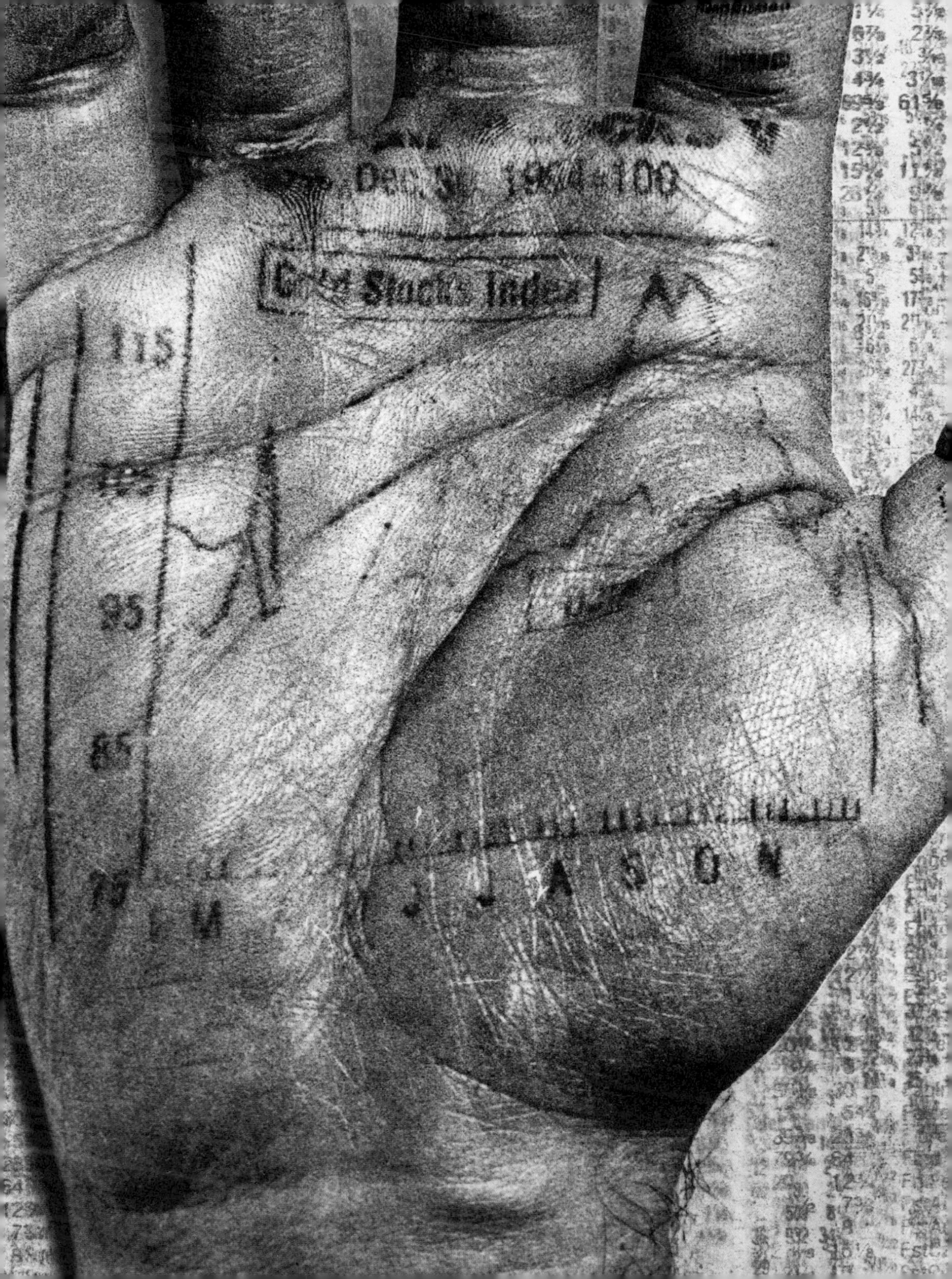
1964=100
115
95
85
A S O N

51200000

The total number of forcibly displaced people across the world in 2013 was 51.2 million (the highest figure since the Second World War). If these people were a nation it would be the 26th largest in the world.

The United Nations Refugee Agency

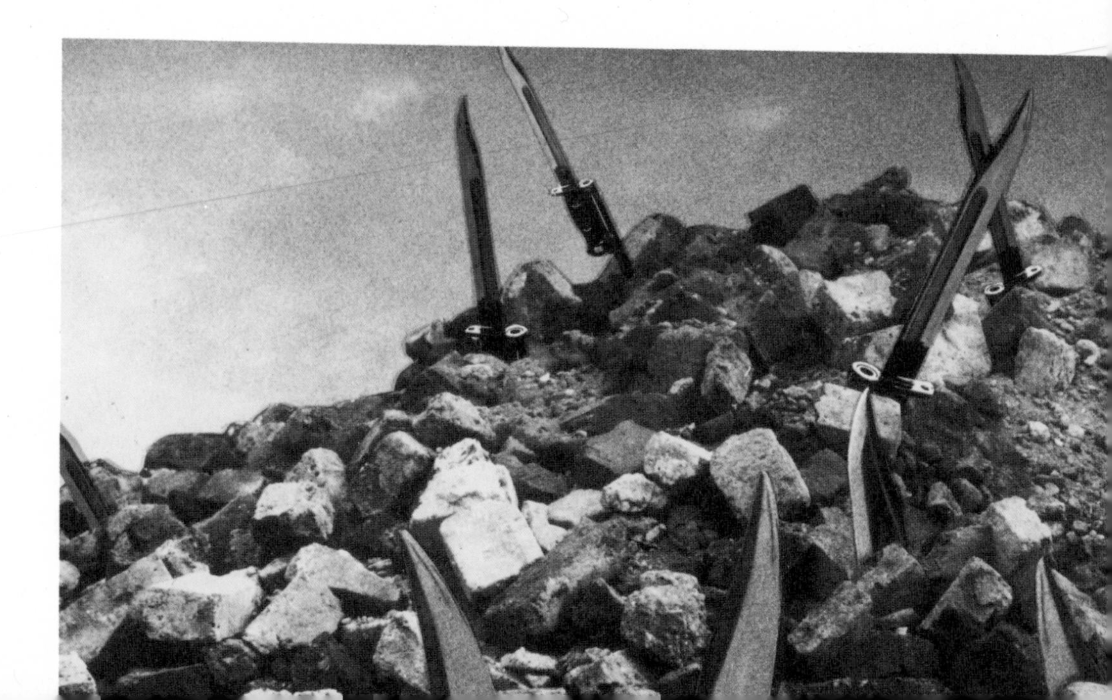

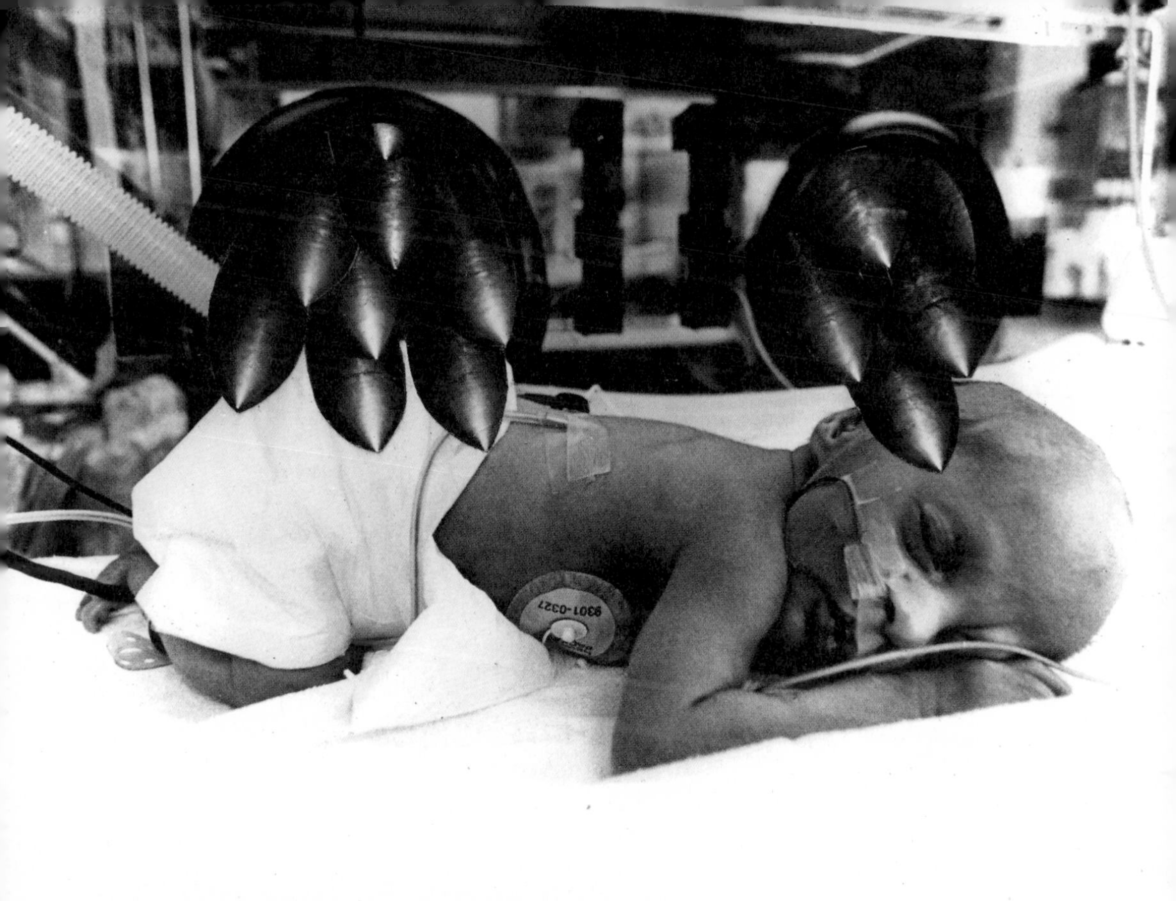
9301-0327

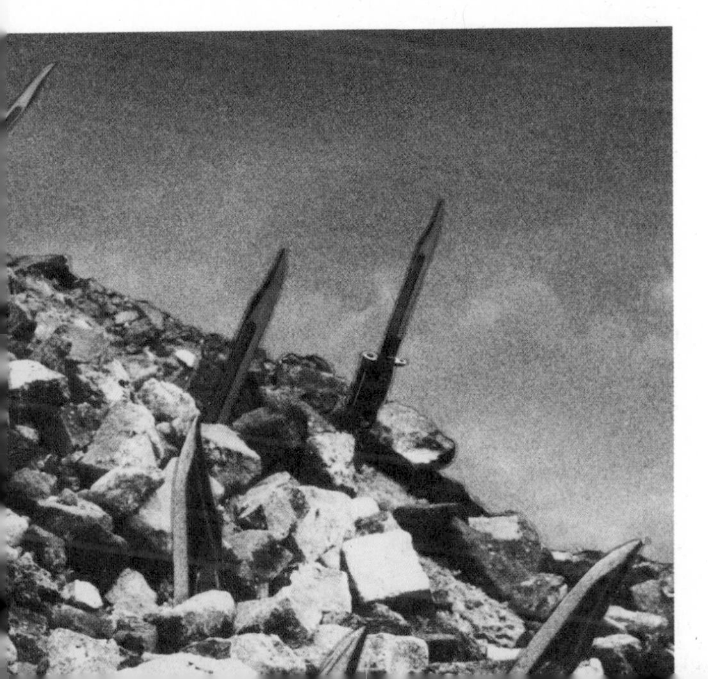

# 1000000000

More than 1 billion people in the world live on less than $1 per day.
Another 2.7 billion struggle to survive on less than $2 per day.

United Nations Millennium Project

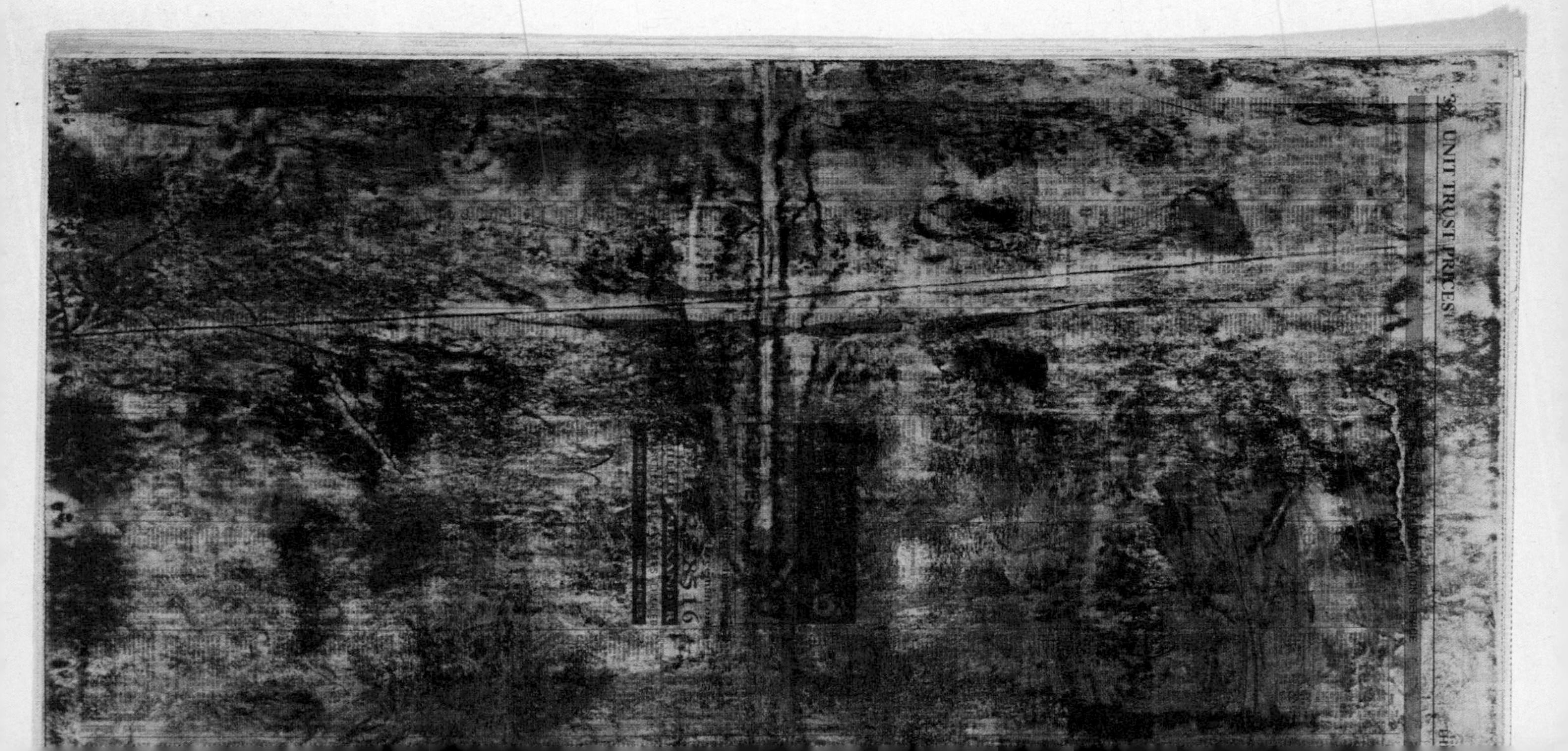

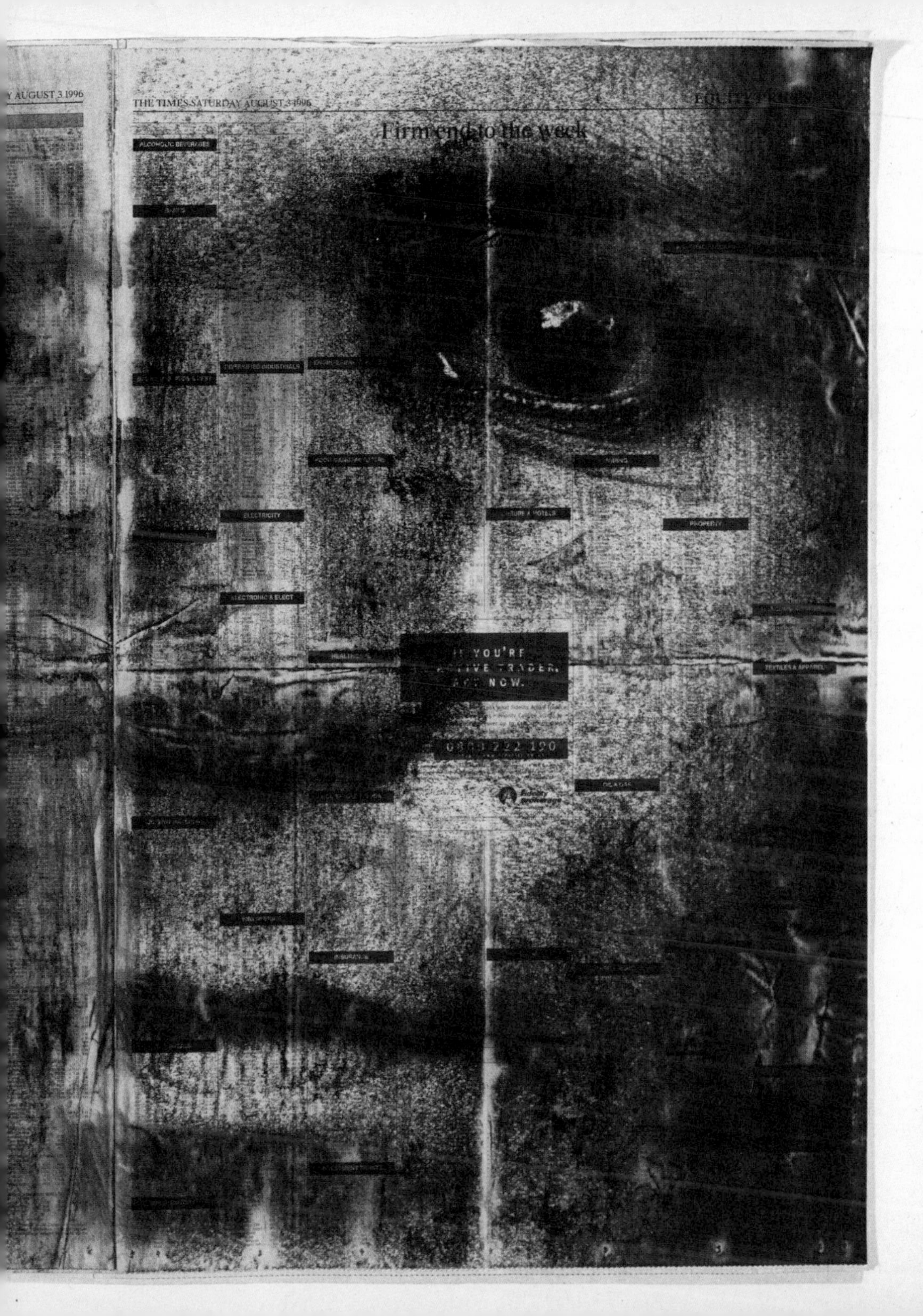

THE TIMES SATURDAY AUGUST 3 1996
Firm end to the week
ALCOHOLIC BEVERAGES
DIVERSIFIED INDUSTRIALS
ELECTRICITY
ELECTRONIC & ELECT
PROPERTY
TEXTILES & APPAREL

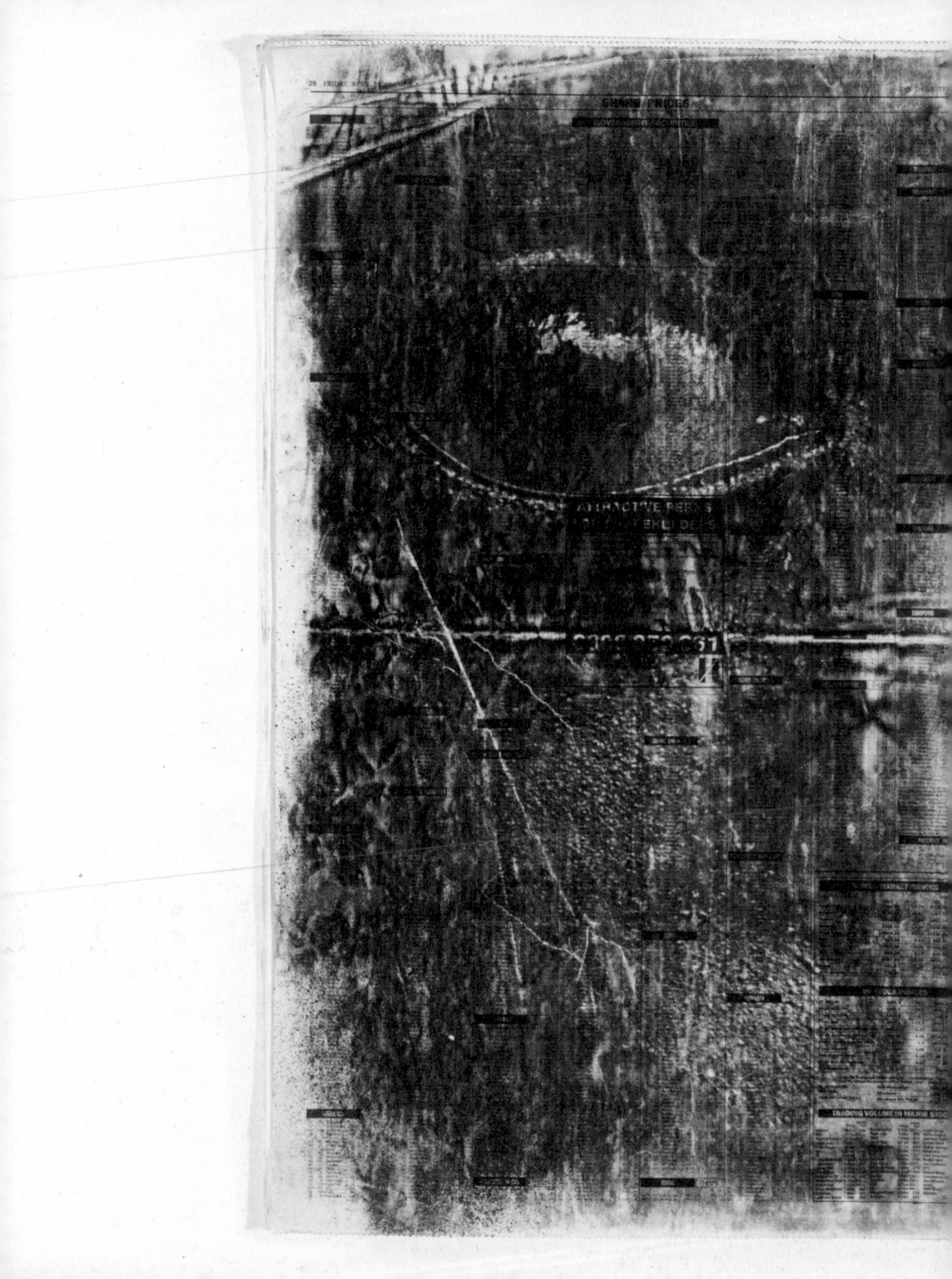

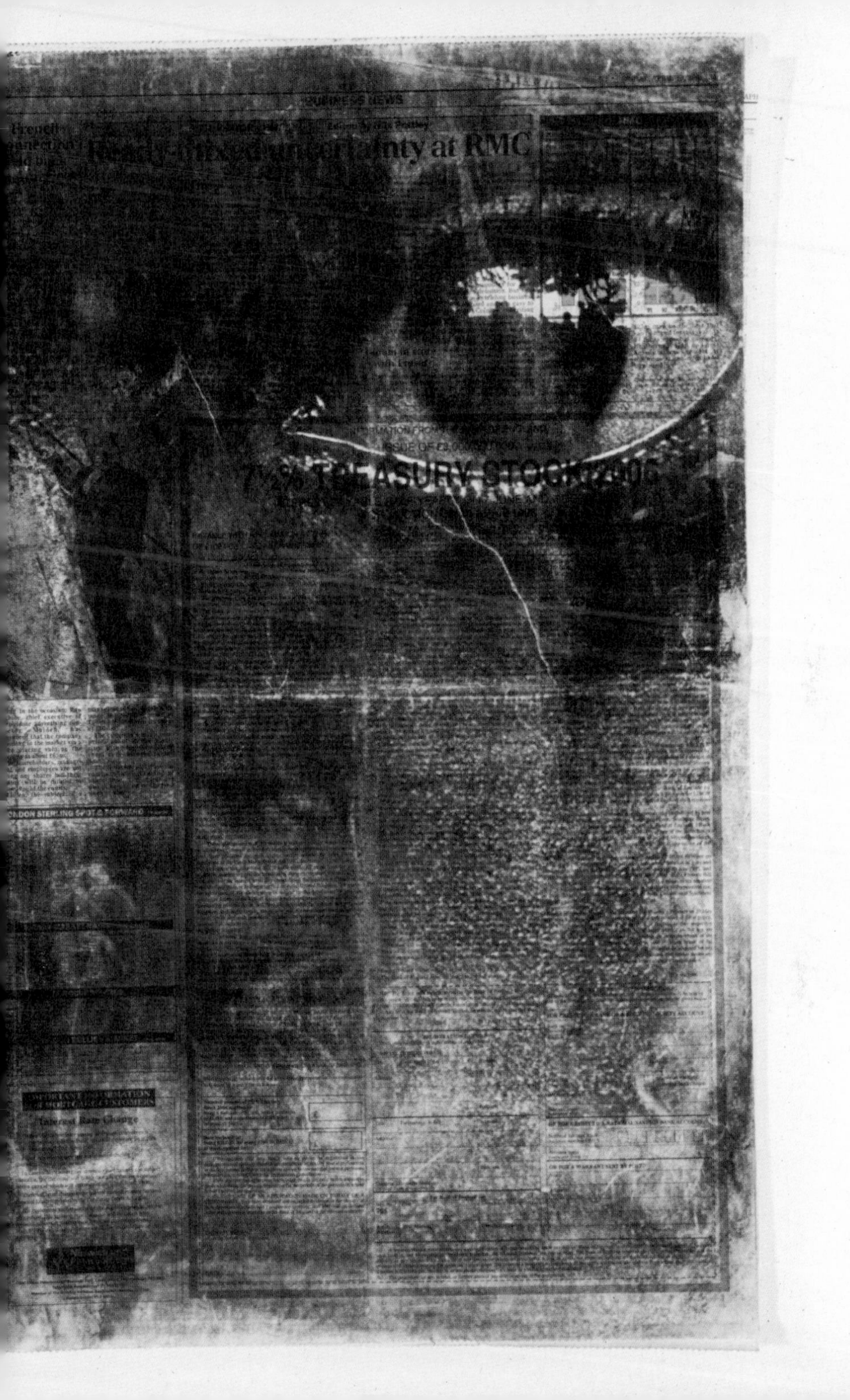

BUSINESS NEWS
TREASURY STOCK

200000 Every year, an estimated 200,000 people die as an indirect result of armed conflict

Amnesty International

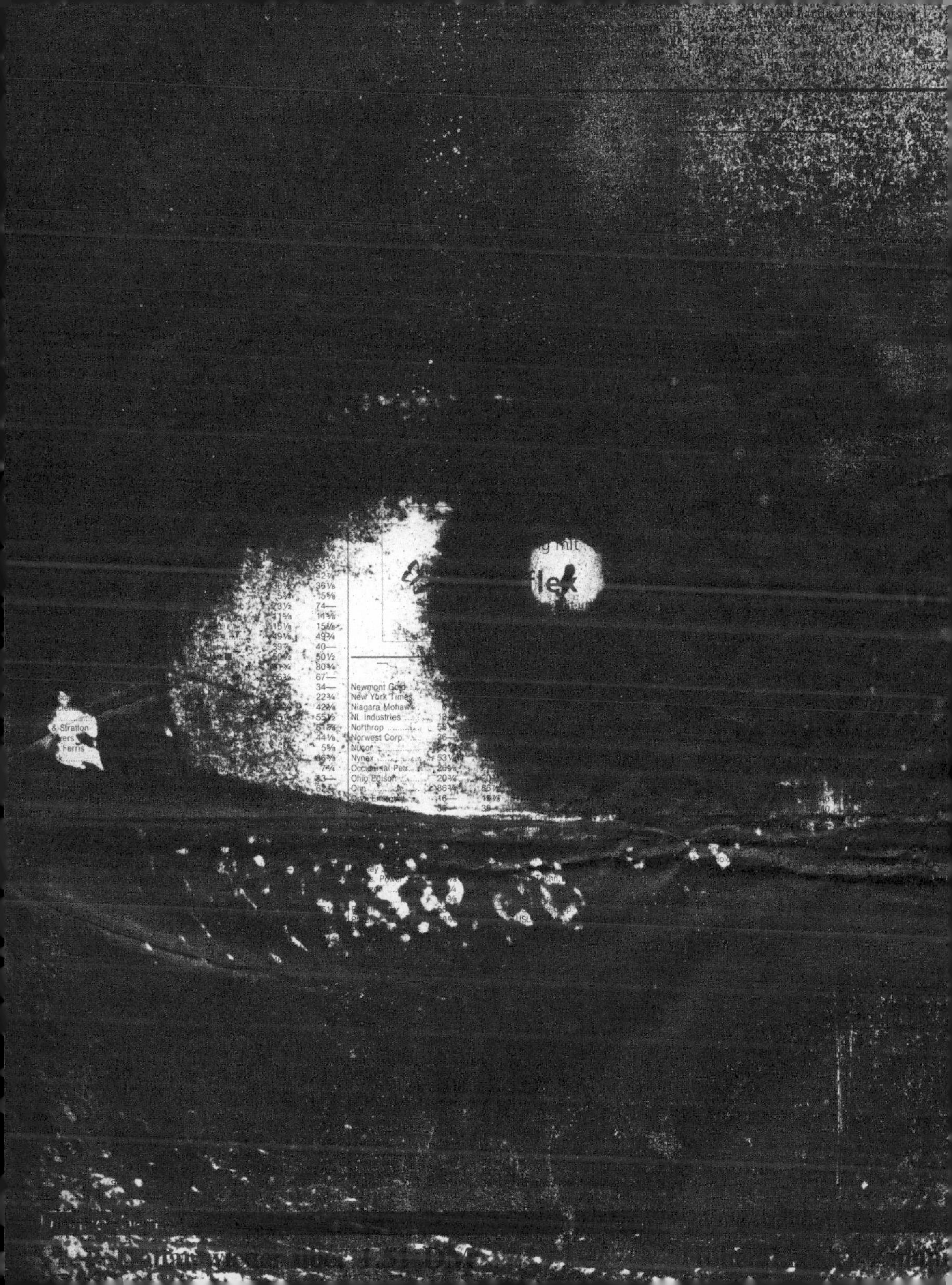

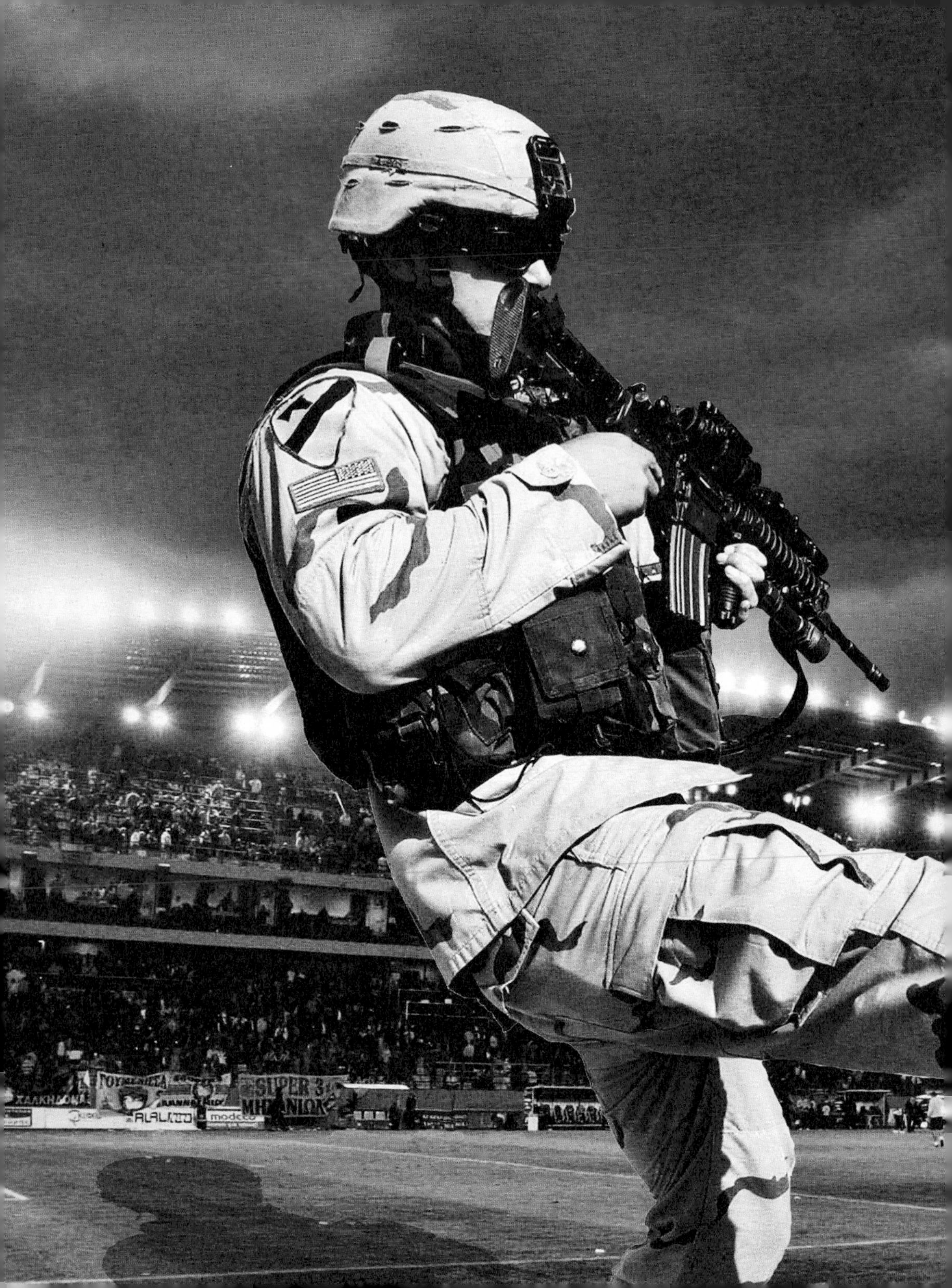
SUPER 3

# 11

The number of nuclear weapons the US has lost and never recovered

Brookings Institute

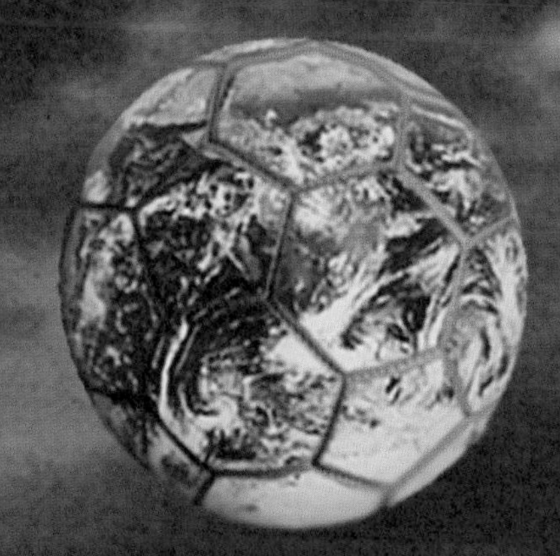

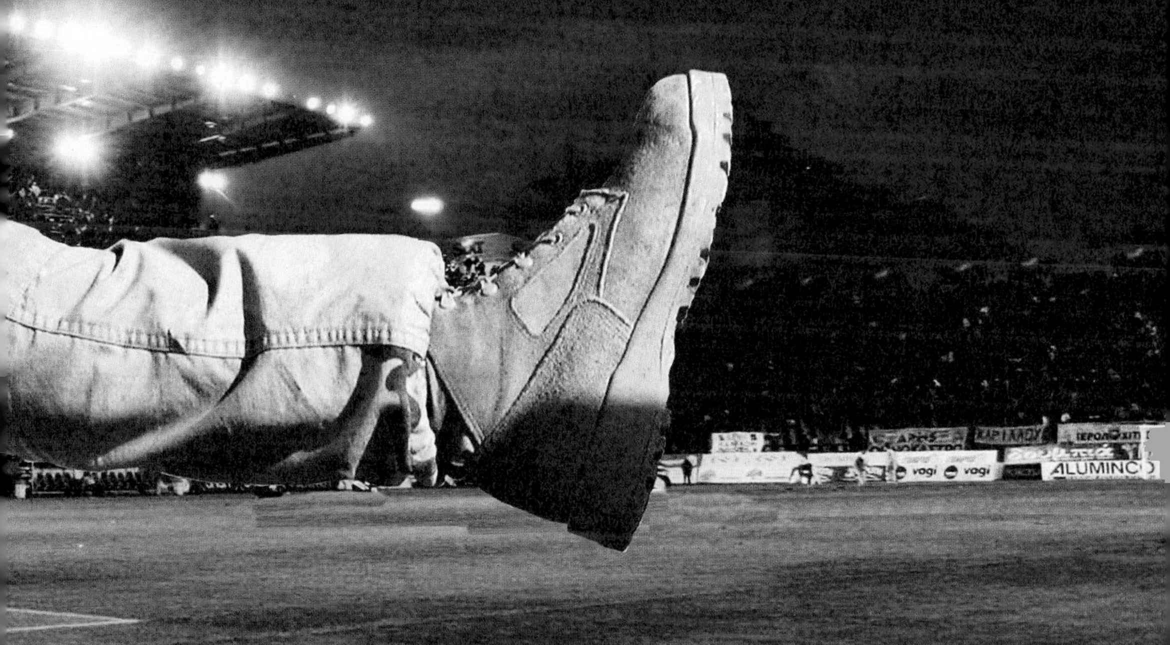

1000000

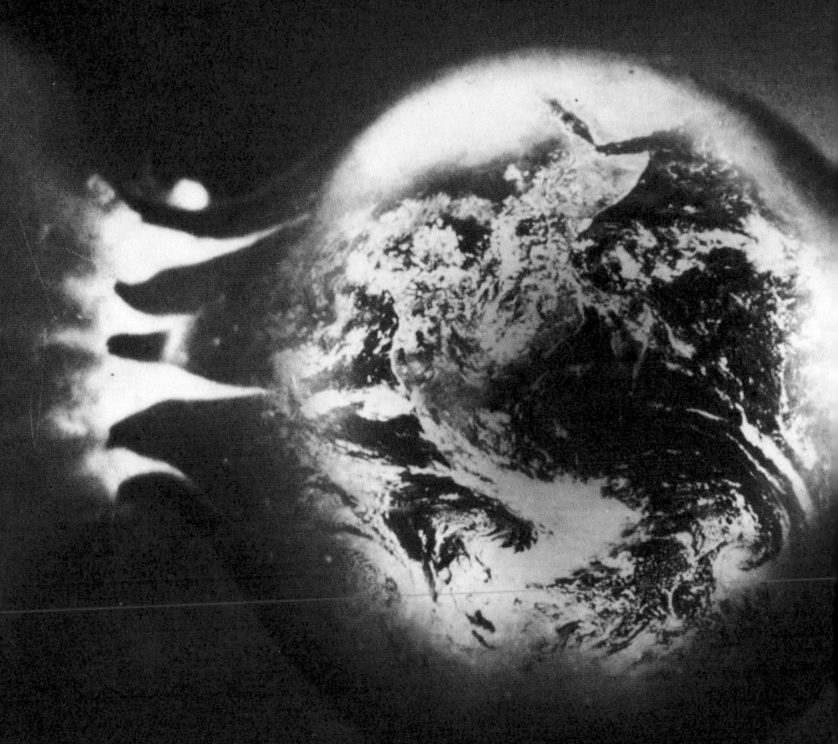

The estimated cost of the modernisation plan for the current US nuclear arsenal, including l

Center for N

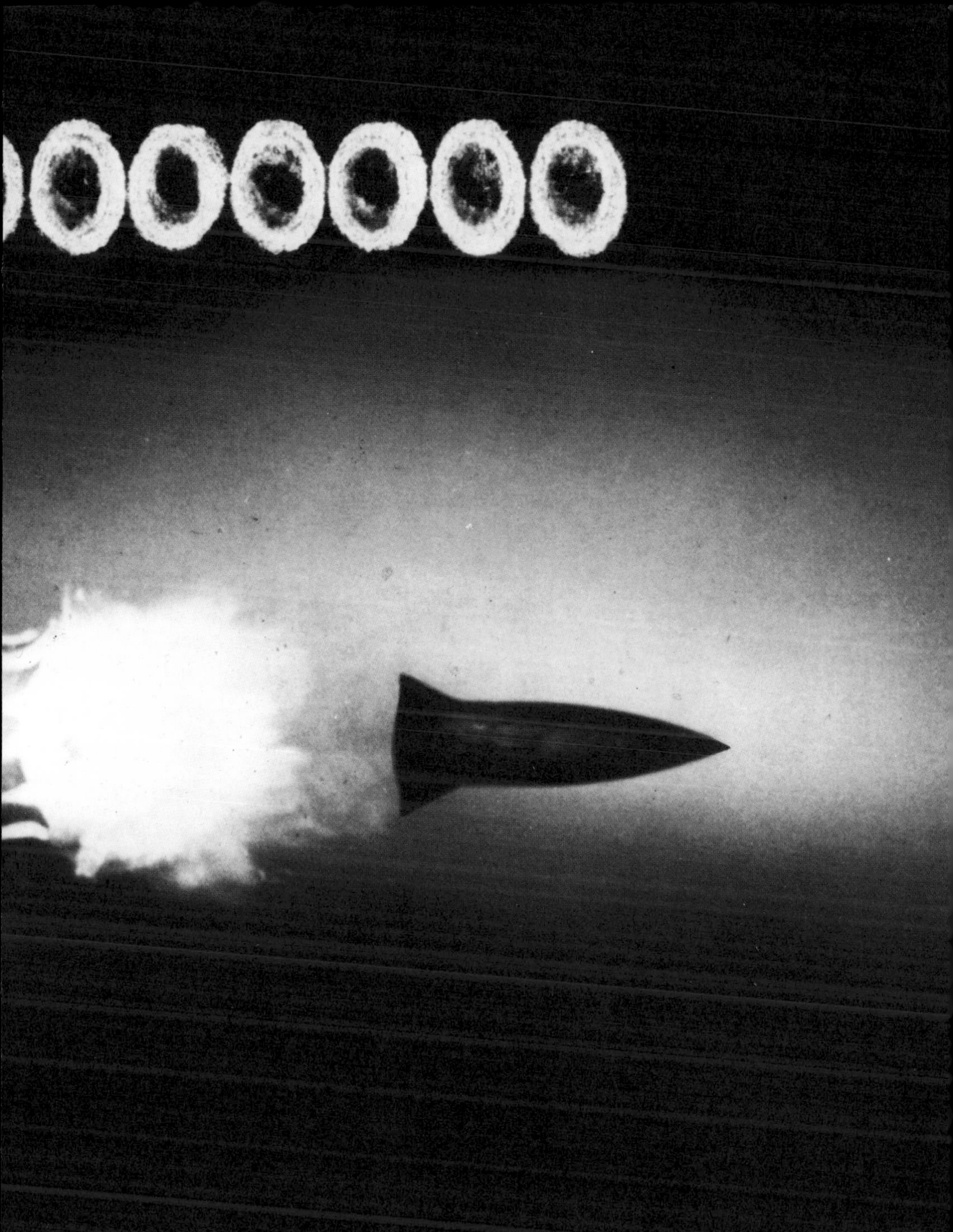

ion programmes for nuclear weapons and procurement of new delivery systems is $1 trillion

ation Studies

# 1000000

A million people gathered in Central Park on June 12, 1982 to demonstrate against nuclear arms and for an end to the arms race

*The Nation*

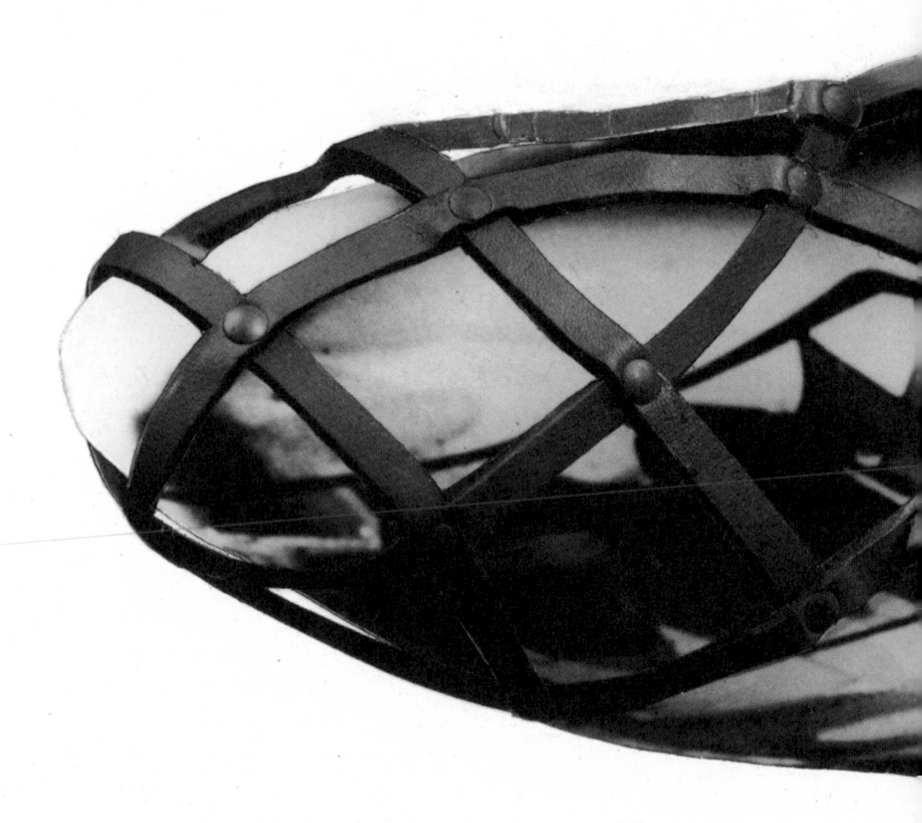

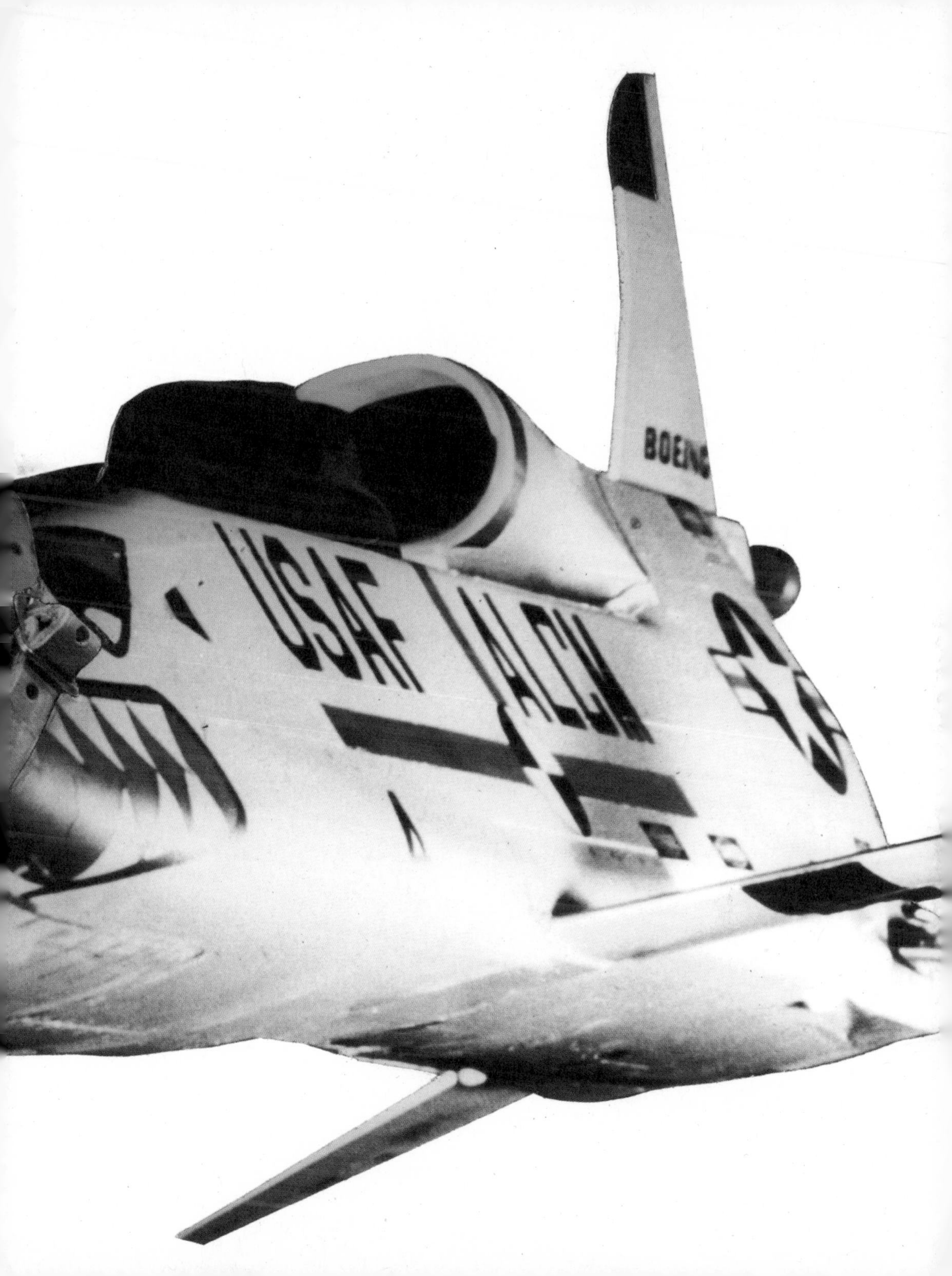
BOEING
USAF
NACA

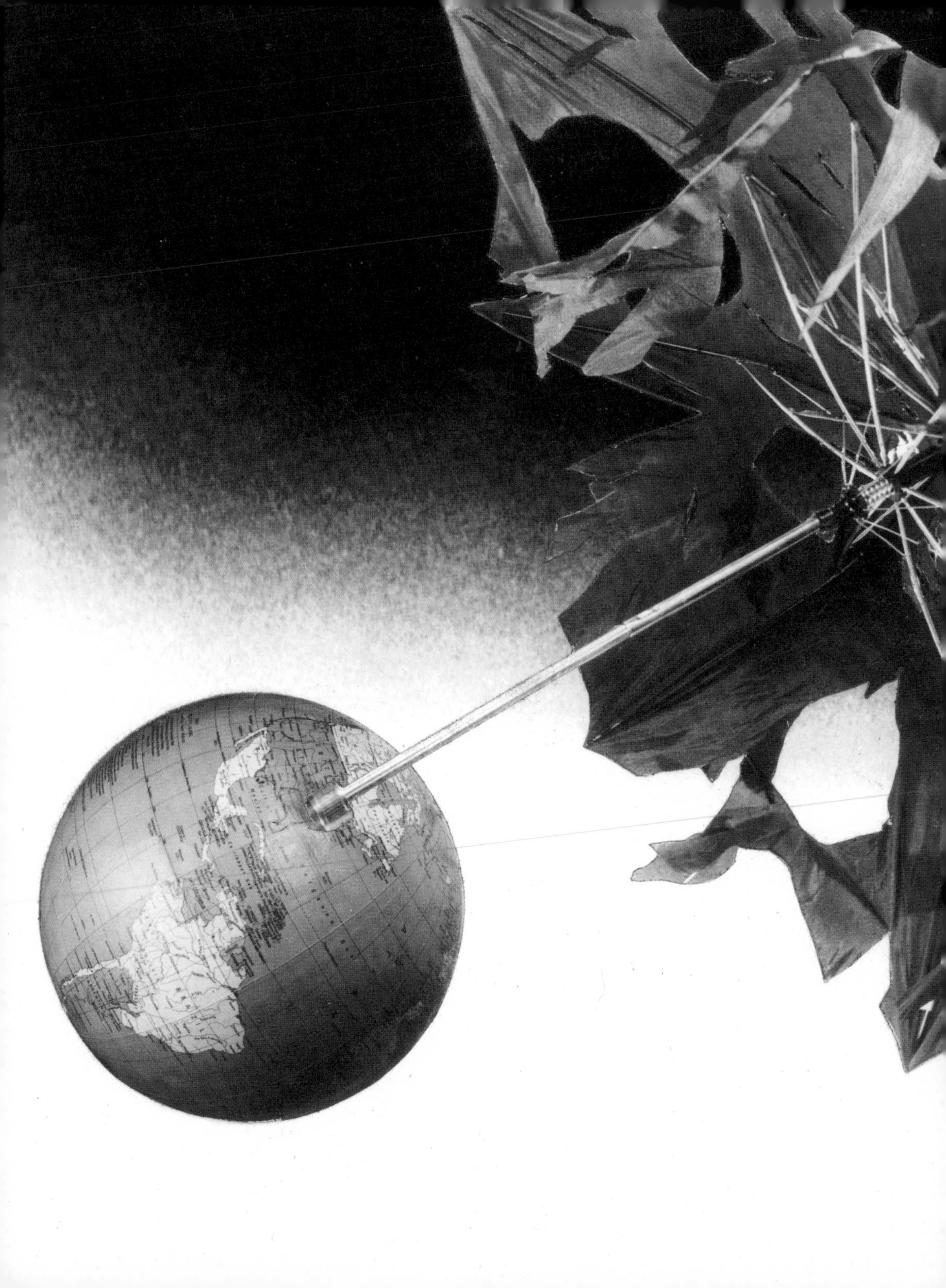

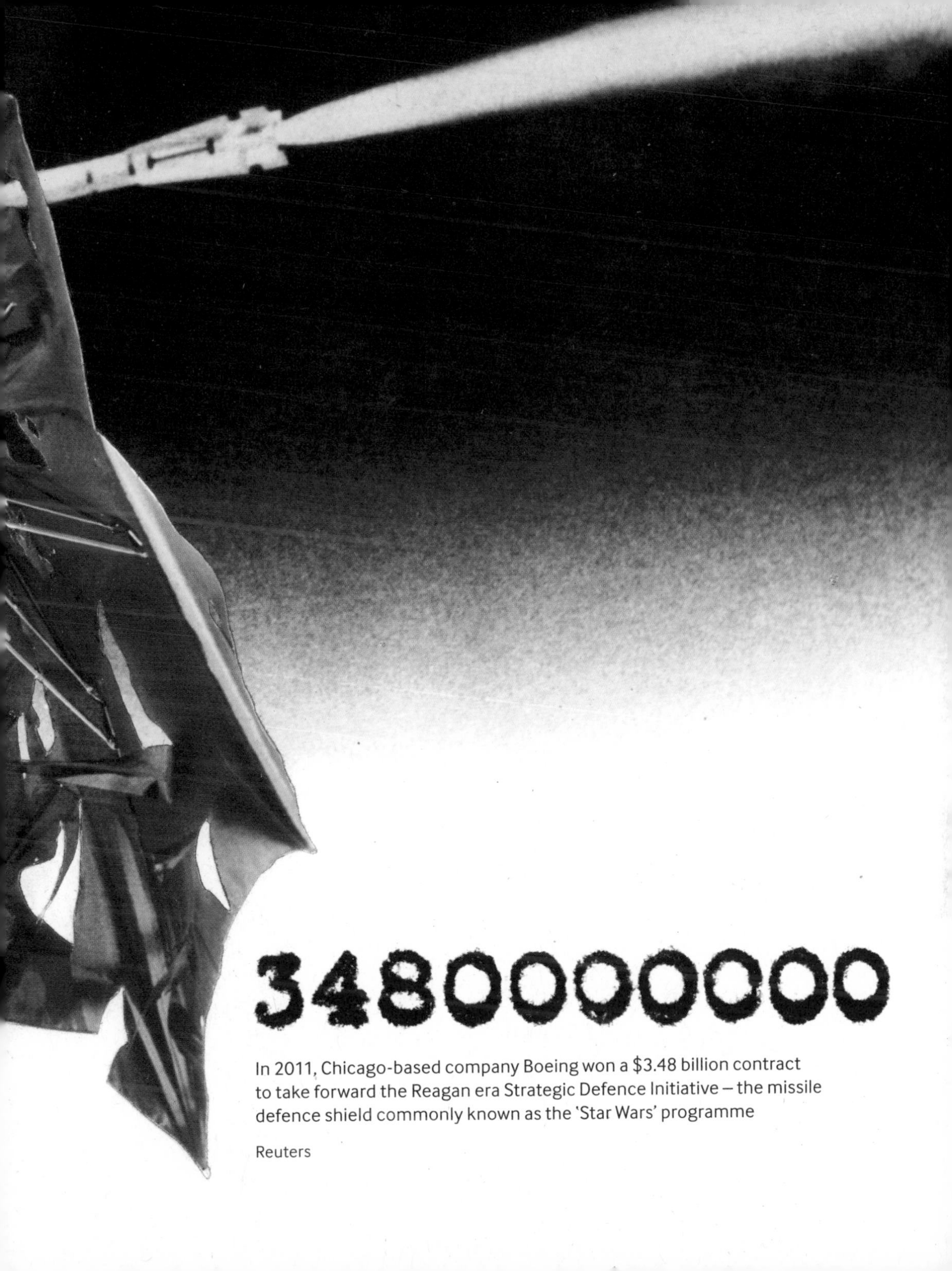

# 3480000000

In 2011, Chicago-based company Boeing won a $3.48 billion contract to take forward the Reagan era Strategic Defence Initiative – the missile defence shield commonly known as the 'Star Wars' programme

Reuters

The richest 85 people in the world own the same amount of wealth as the poorest half of humanity, 3.5 billion people

Oxfam

85

3500000000

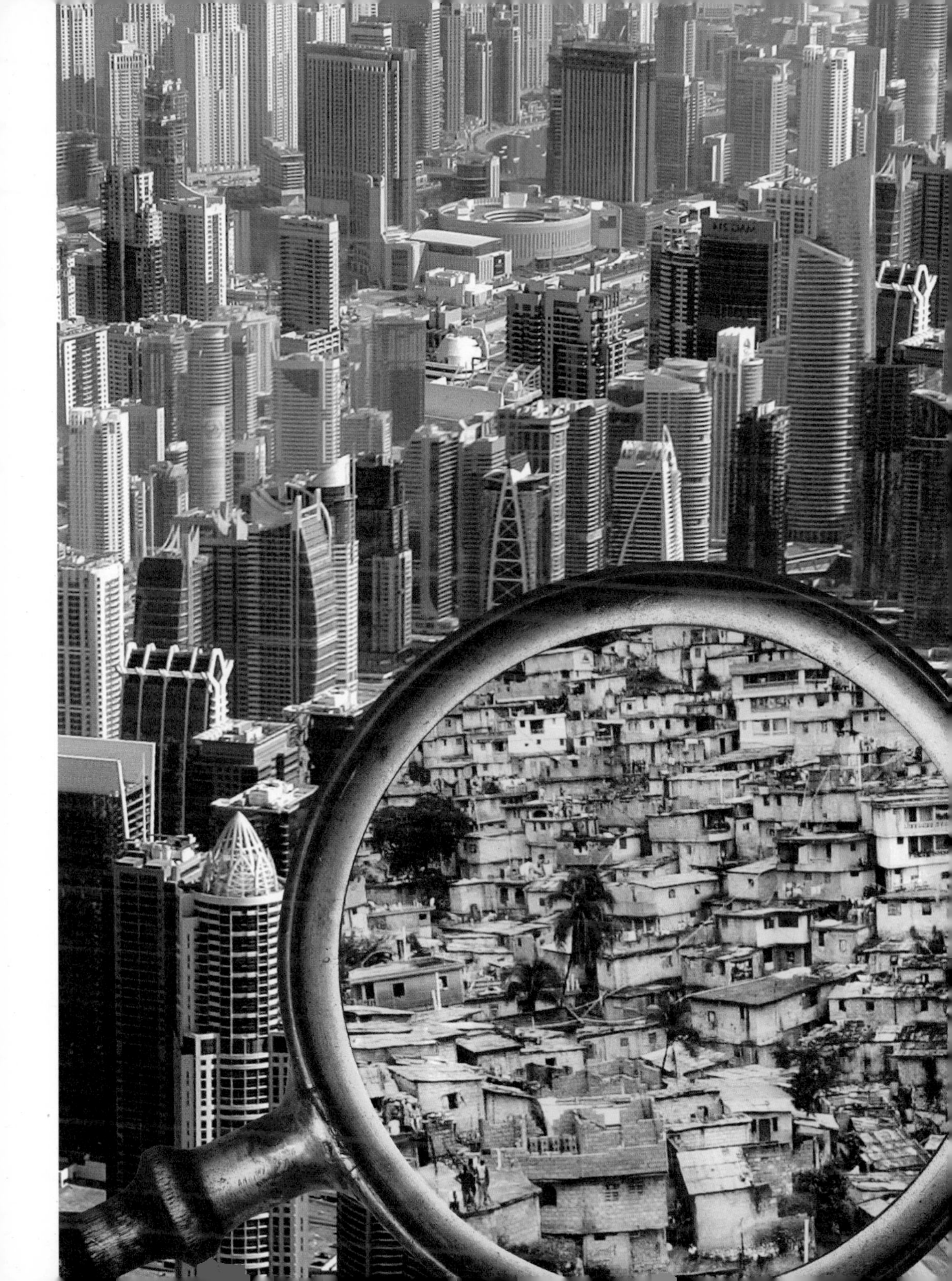

# 7300000000000

It is estimated that the US military spent $7.3 trillion on operations in the Middle East between 1976 and 2007

Department of Near Eastern Studies, Princeton University

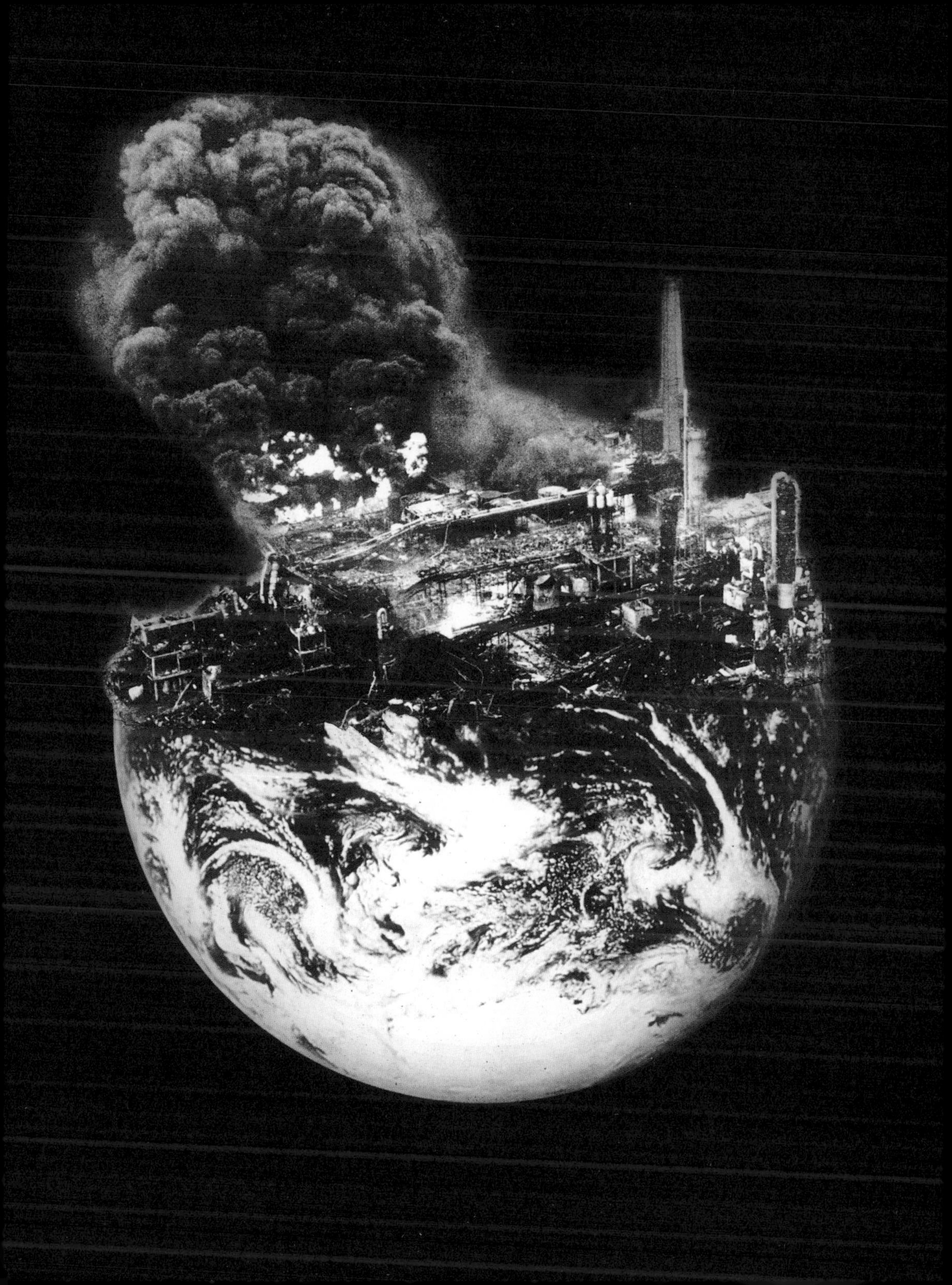

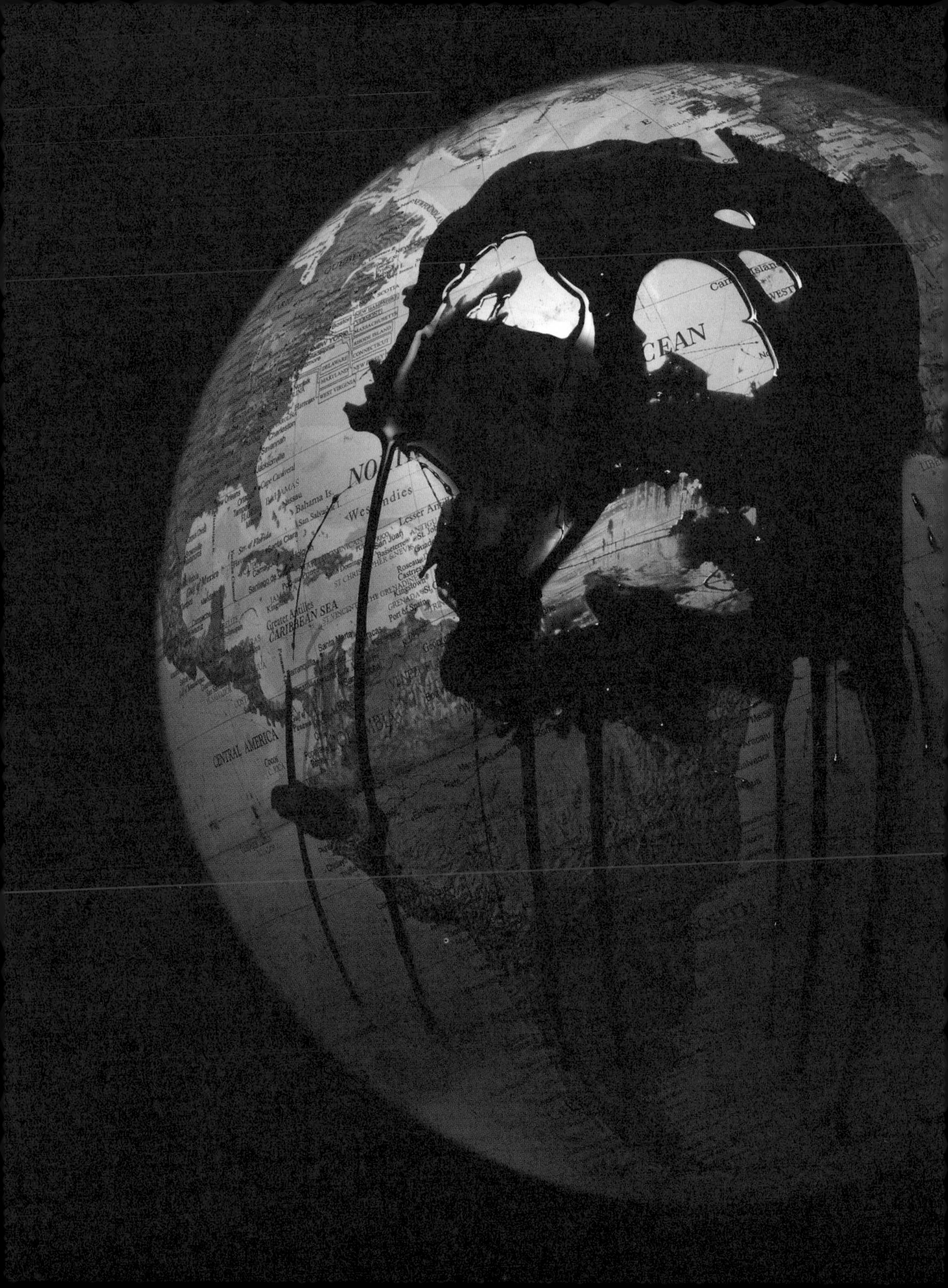

CEAN
NORTH
West Indies
Bahama Is.
San Salvador
Lesser Antilles
Greater Antilles
CARIBBEAN SEA
CENTRAL AMERICA
NEW YORK
MASSACHUSETTS
RHODE ISLAND
CONNECTICUT
DELAWARE
MARYLAND
WEST VIRGINIA
Kingstown
Port of Spain
Roseau
Castries
Santo Domingo

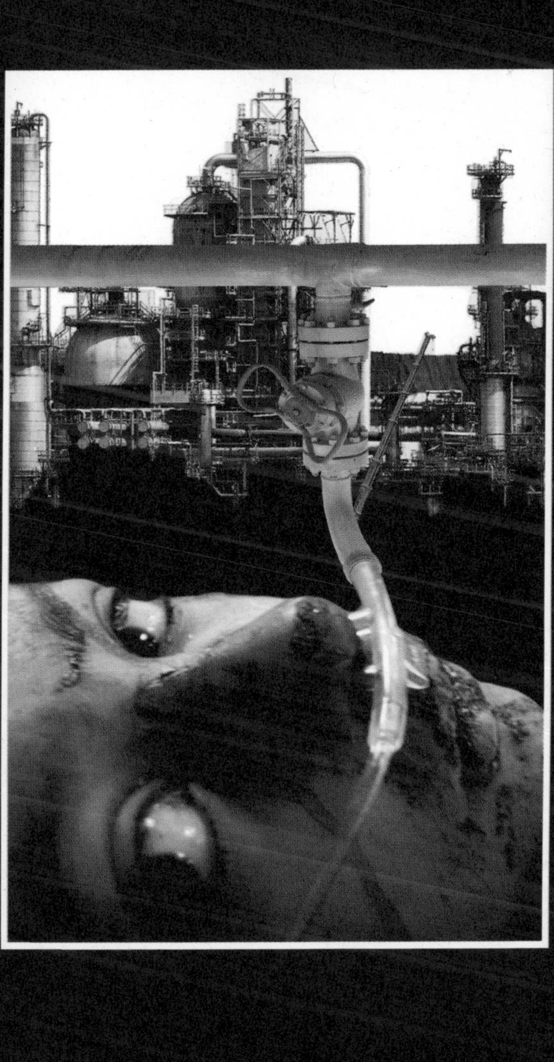

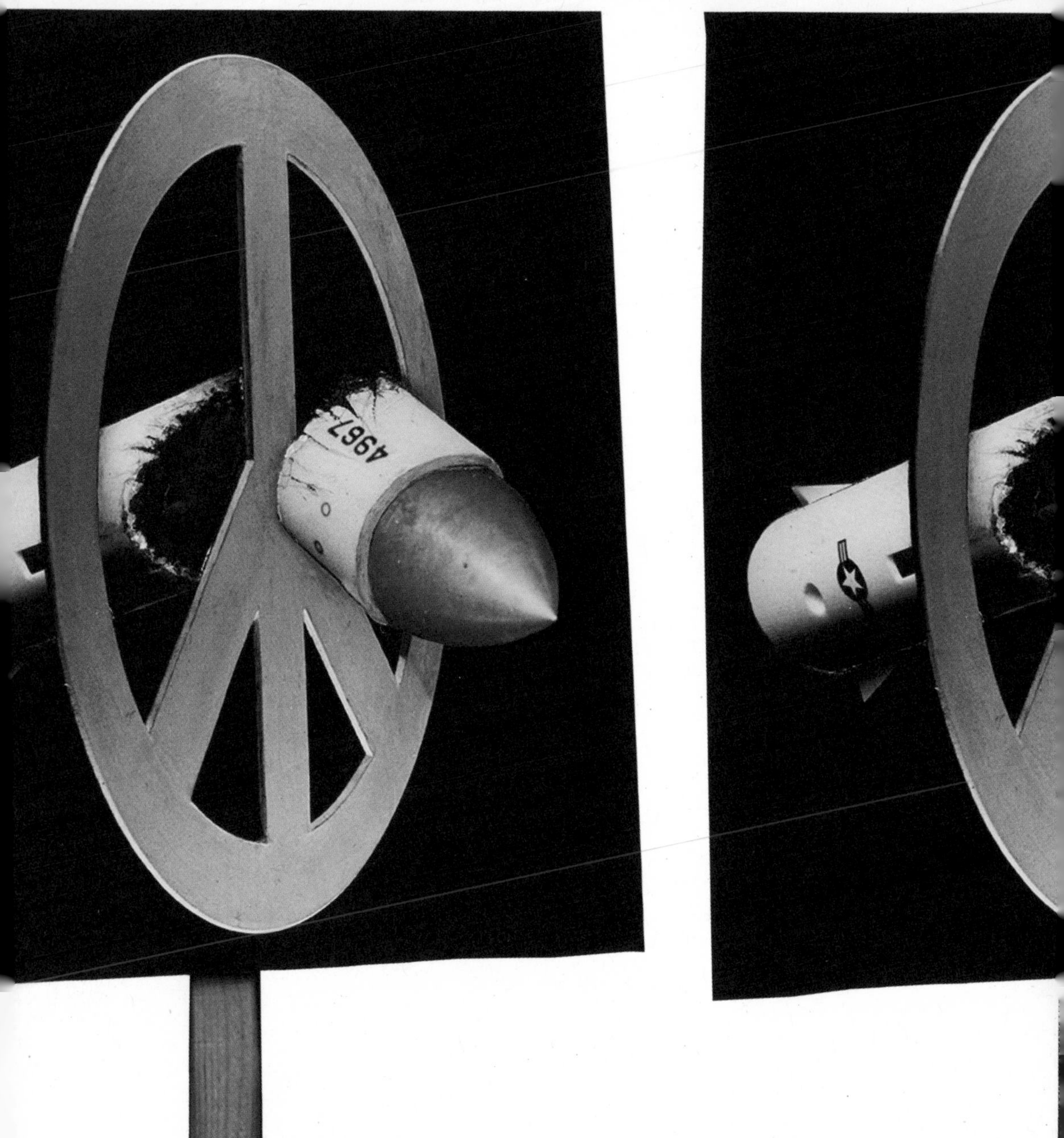


30000000

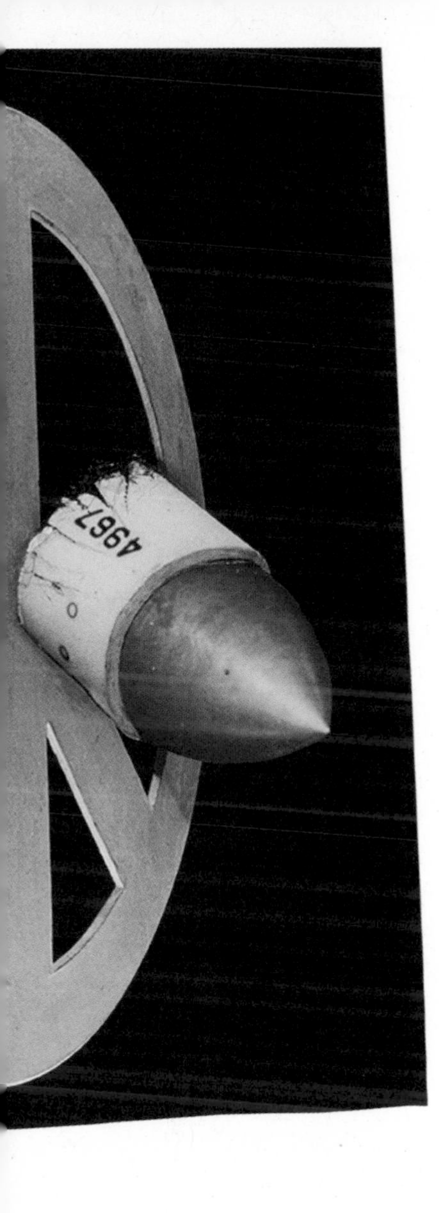



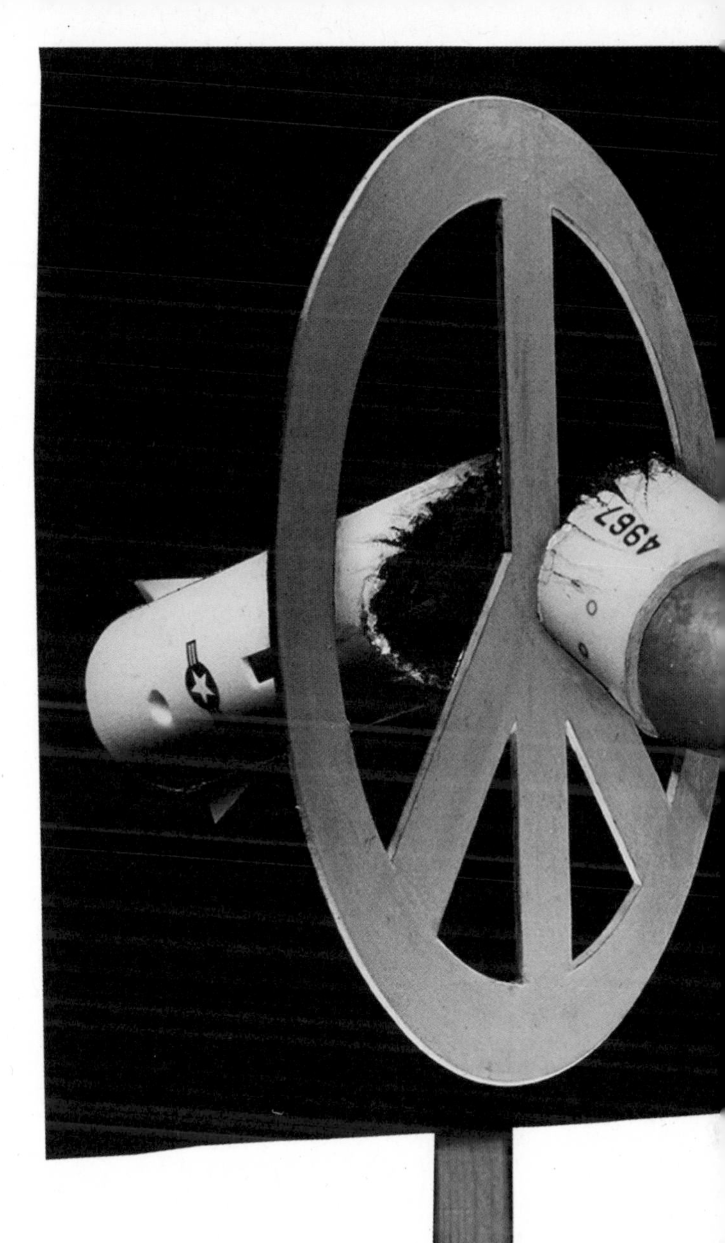



On 15 February 2003 demonstrations against the invasion of Iraq were held in over 600 cities around the world. An estimated 30 million people marched in the largest co-ordinated demonstration against war in history.

*Guardian*

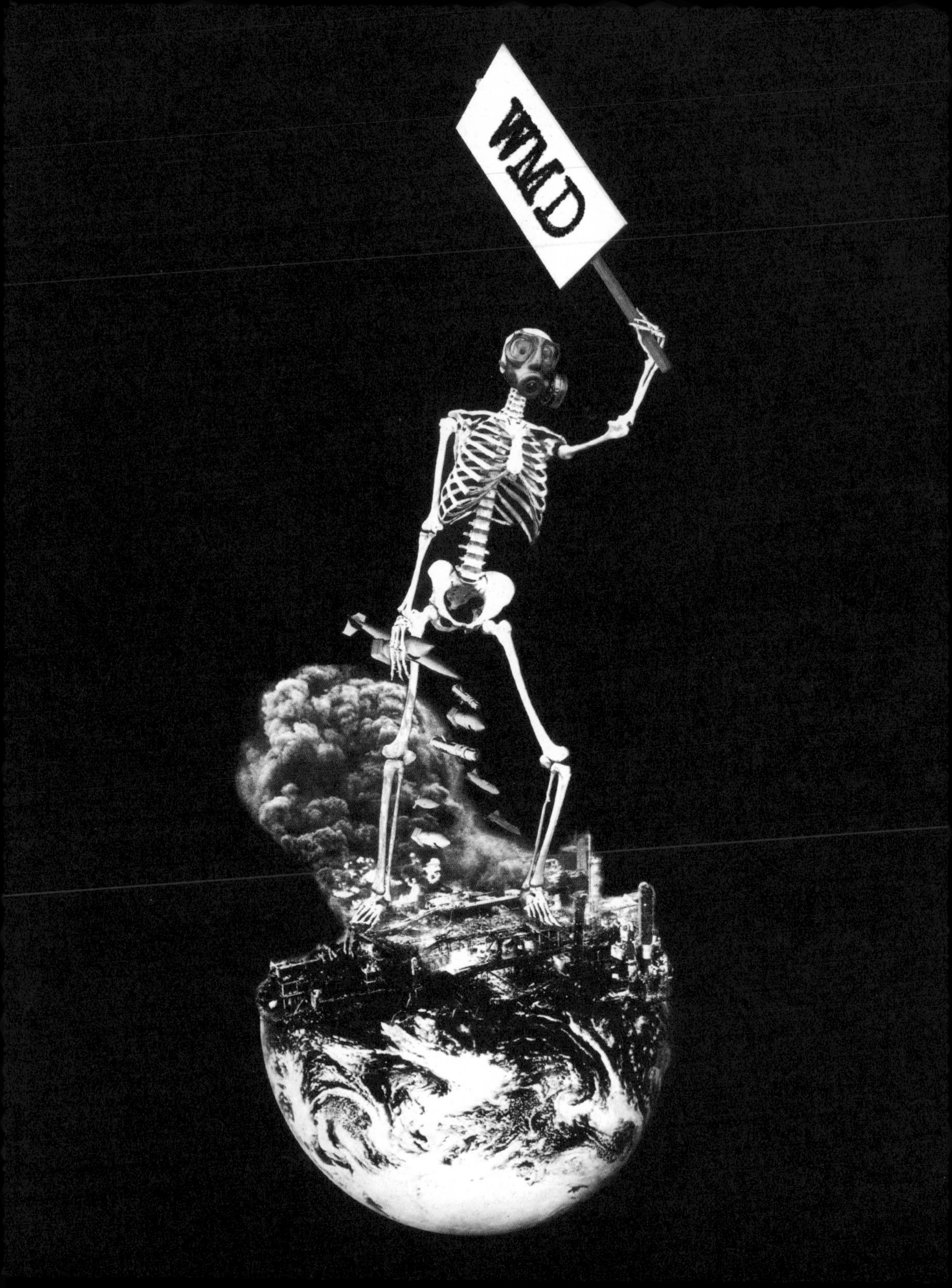
WMD

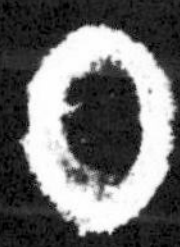


The number of
Weapons of Mass Destruction
(WMDs)
found in Iraq

There were 4,807 US and Allied Coalition military fatalities in Iraq between 2003 and 2014

Iraq Coalition Casualty Count

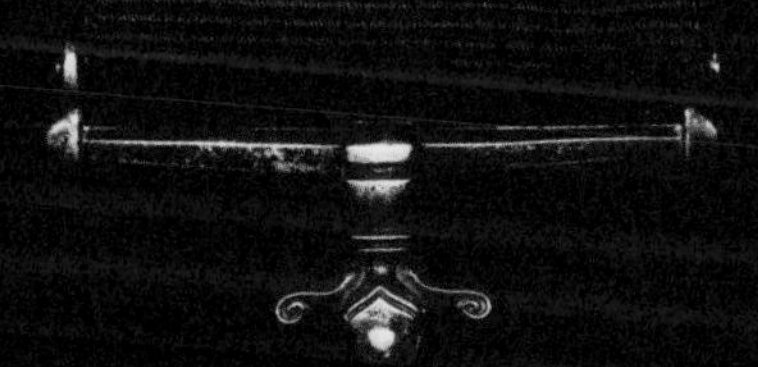

# 654965

Three years after the invasion of Iraq, the medical journal *The Lancet* estimated that 654,965 Iraqi deaths had resulted from the invasion and occupation between 2003 and 2006 (2.5 per cent of the population). There are no official figures from the Coalition, who do not publicly account for enemy or civilian deaths.

*The Lancet*

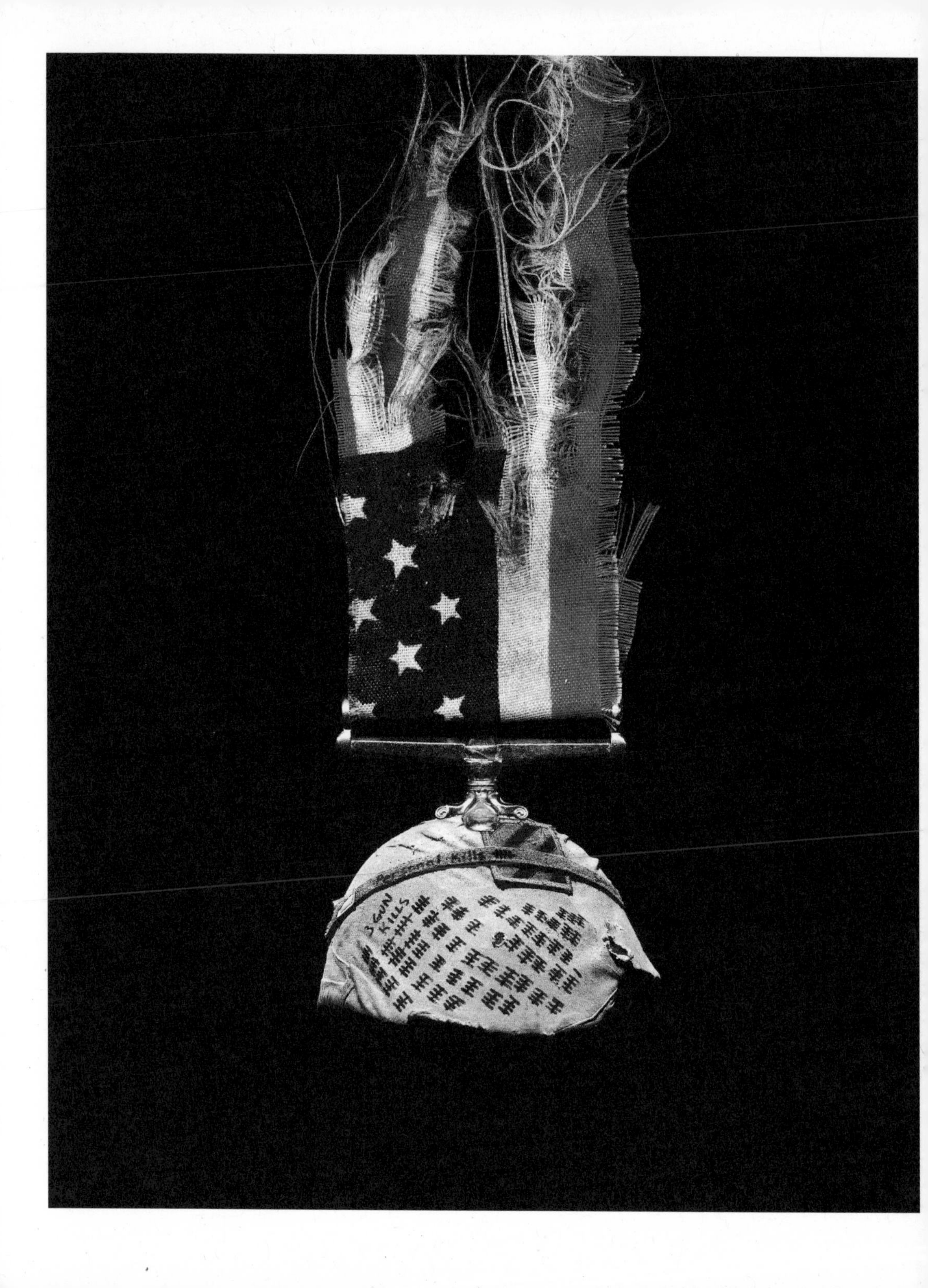
3GUN
KILLS

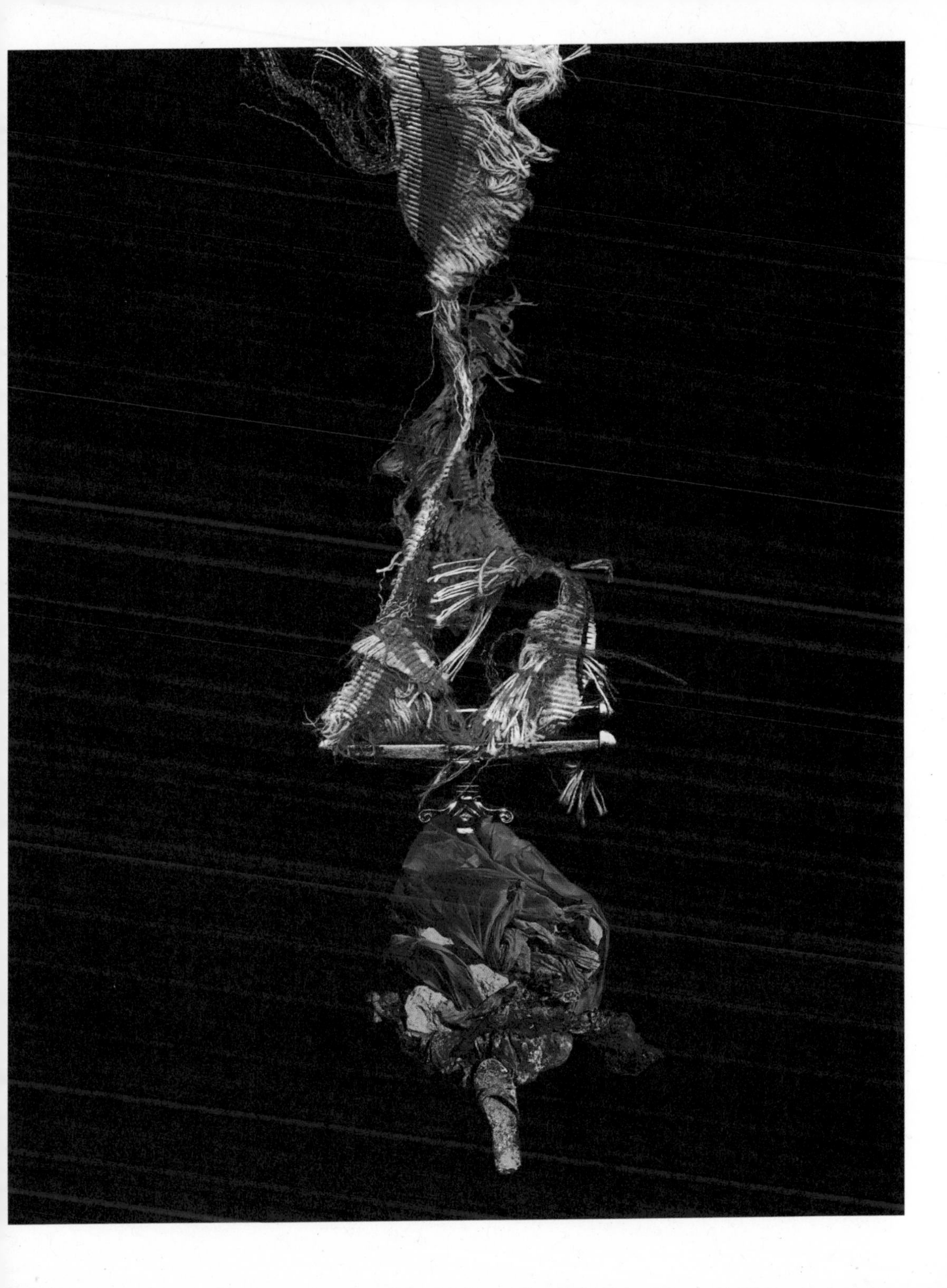

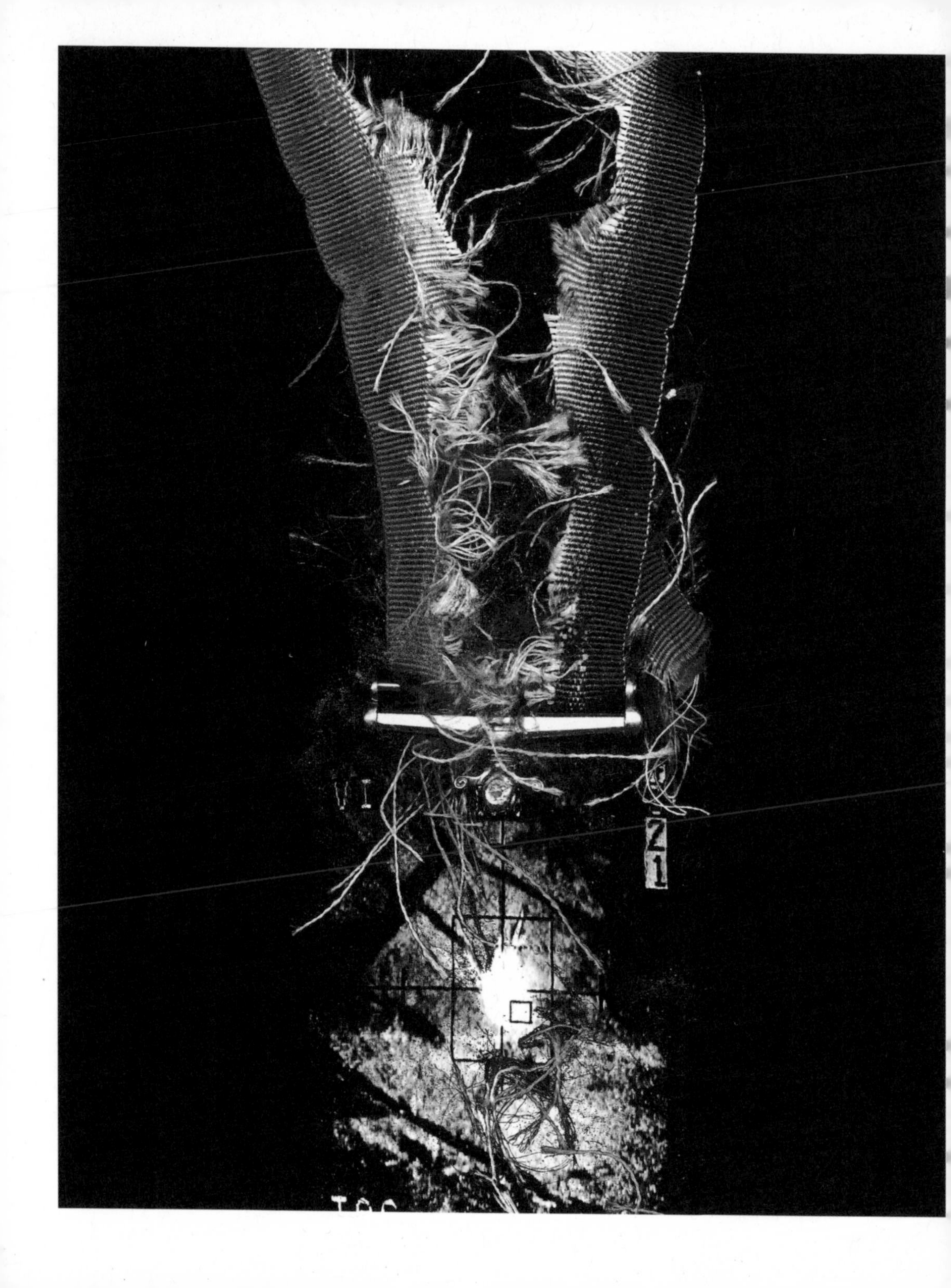

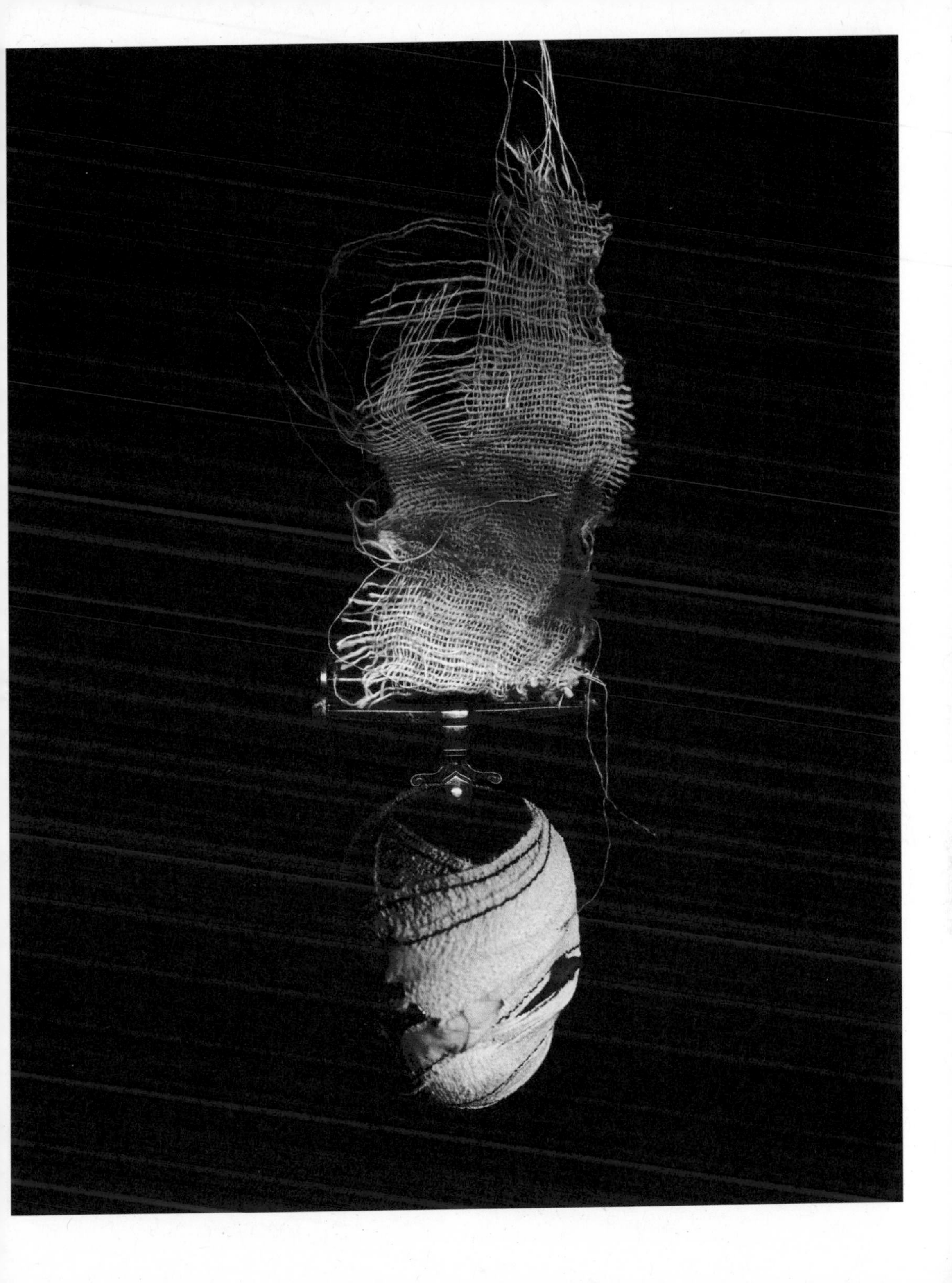

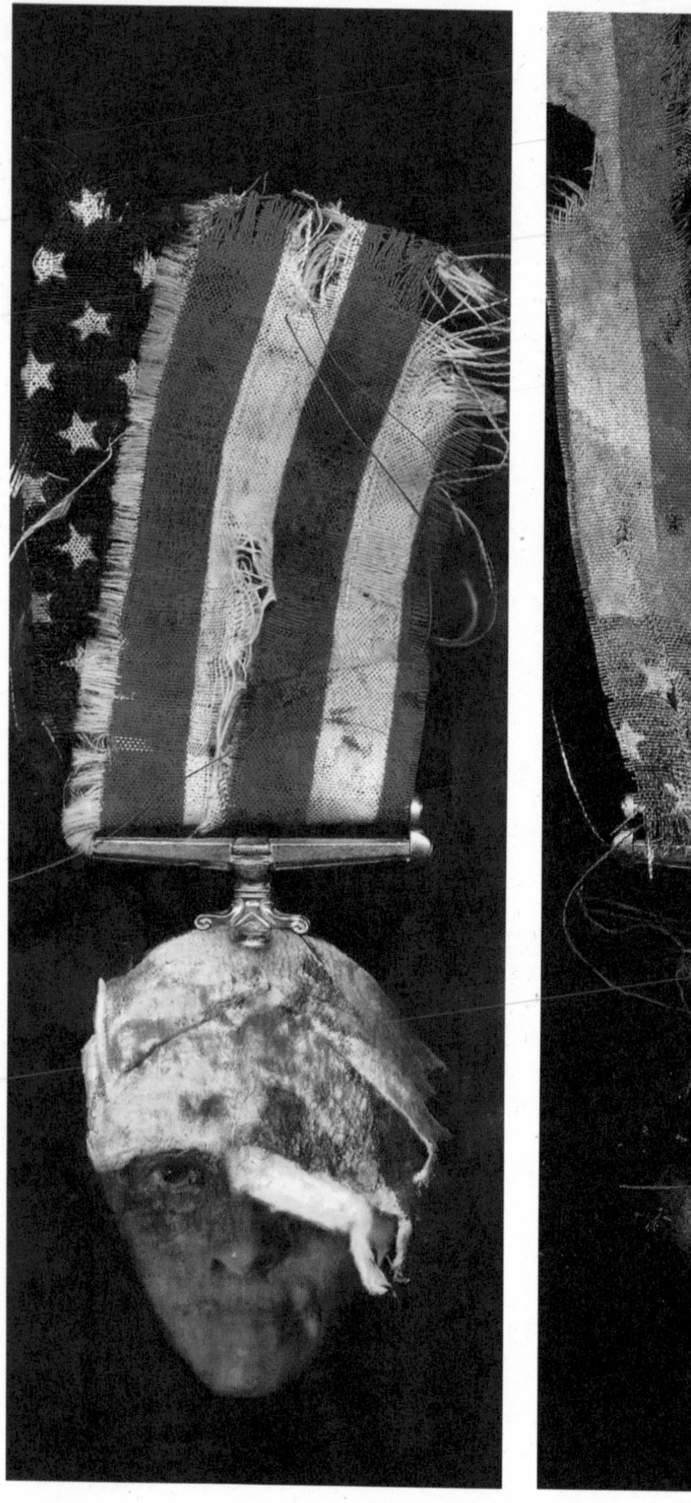
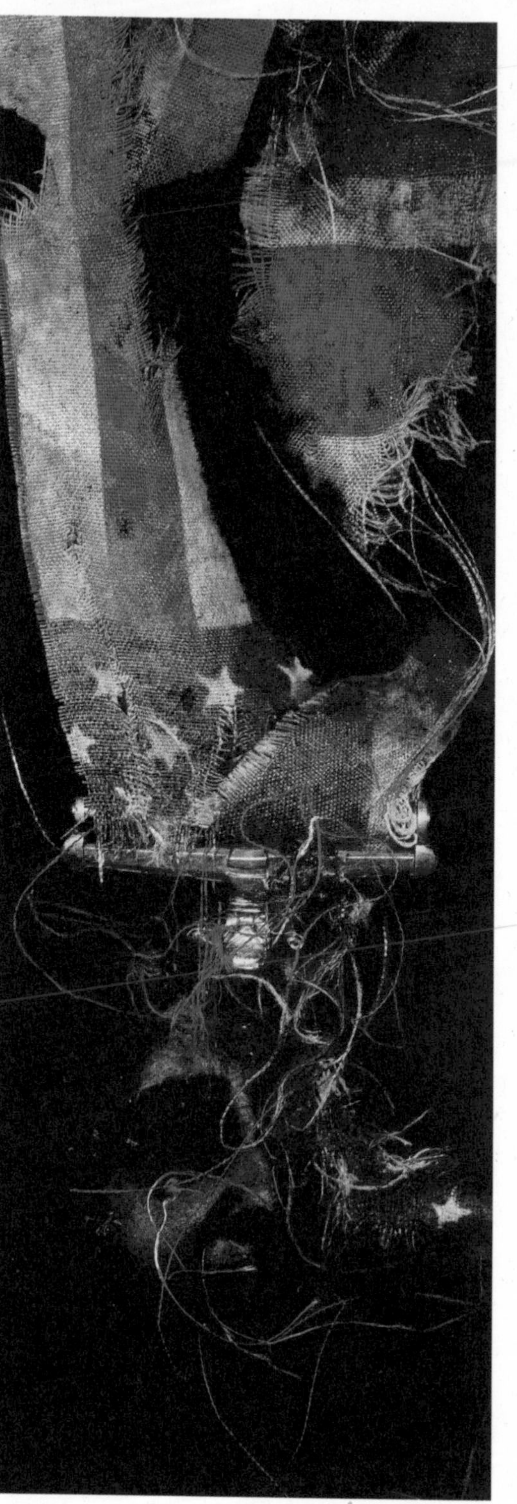

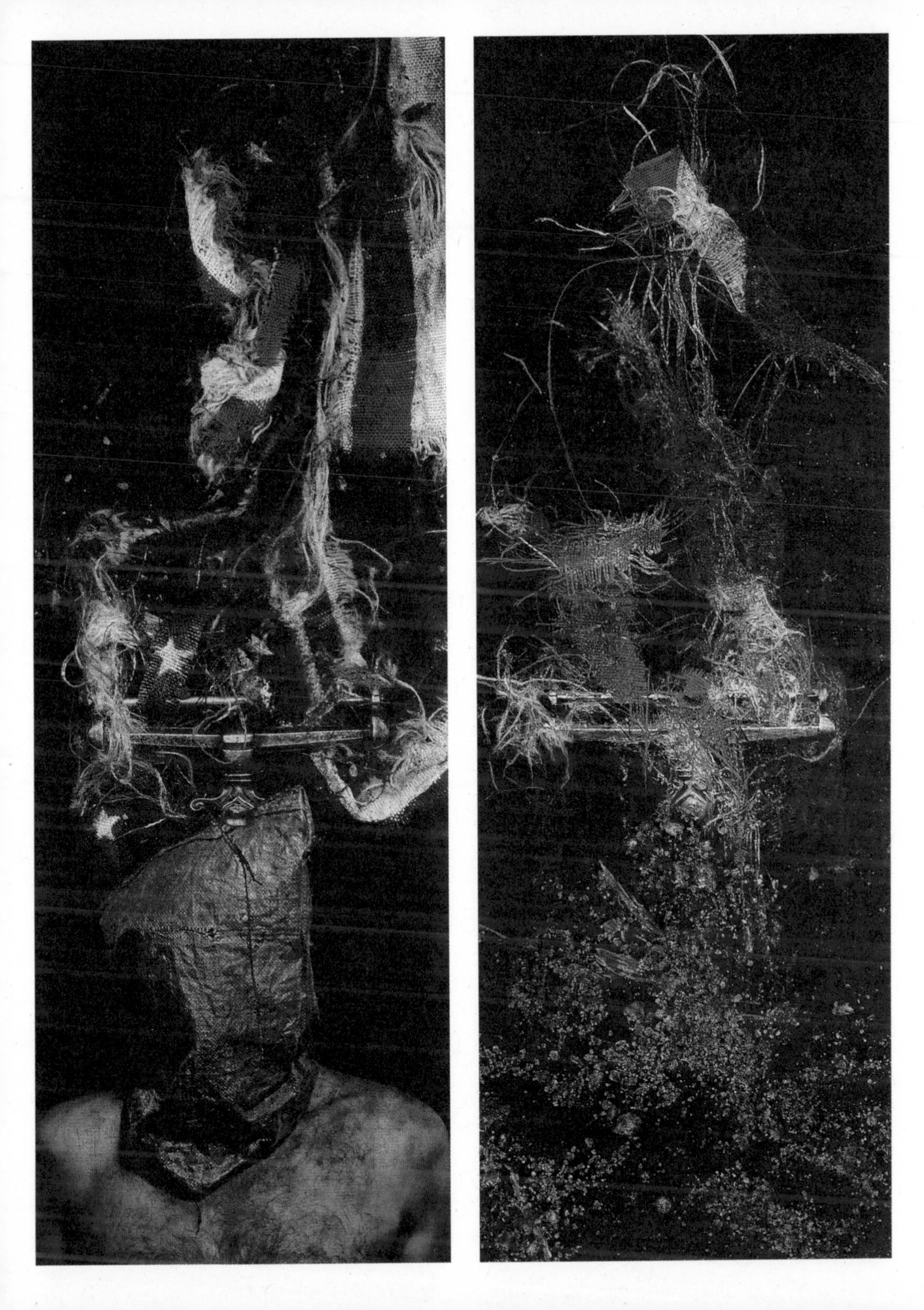

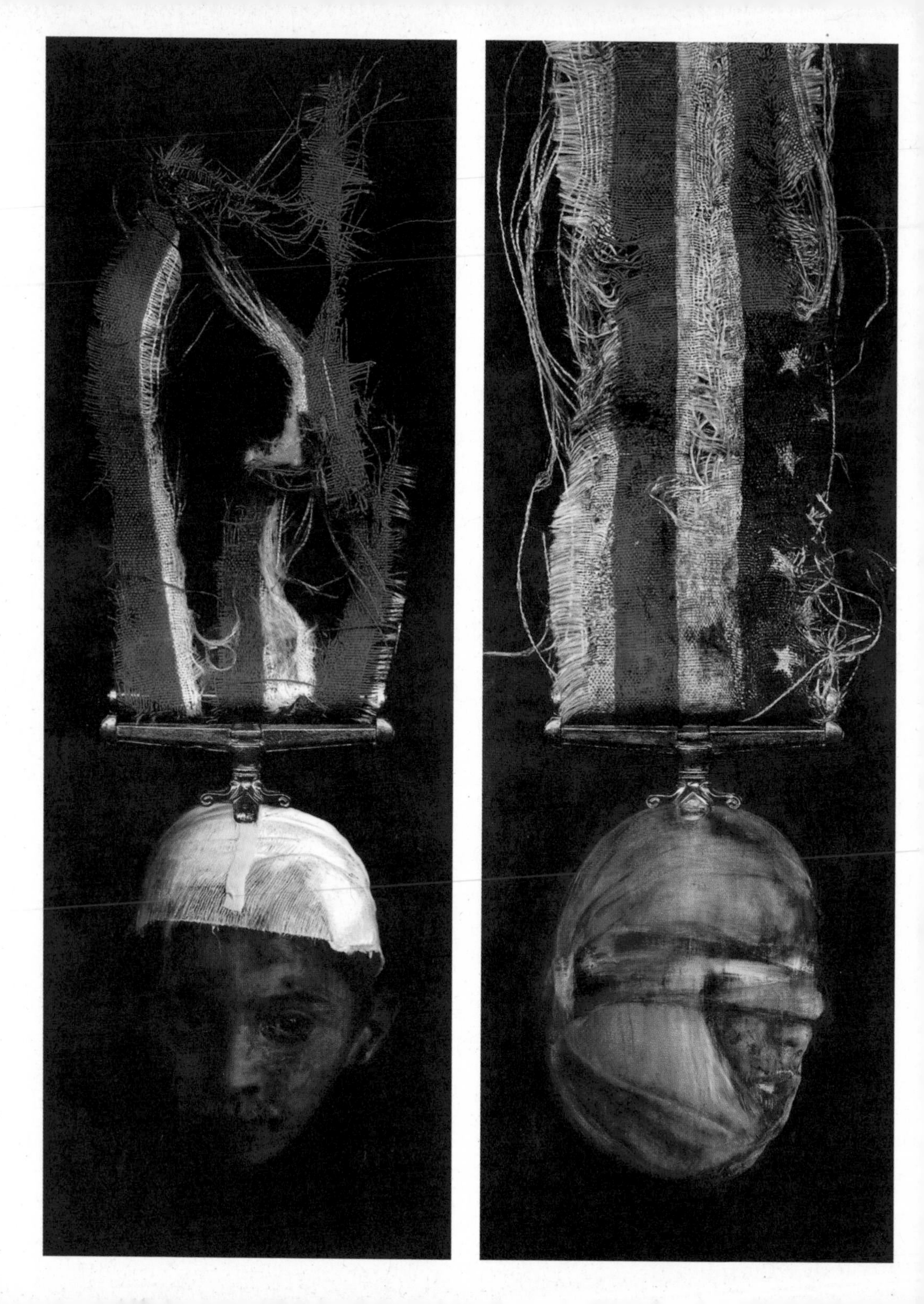

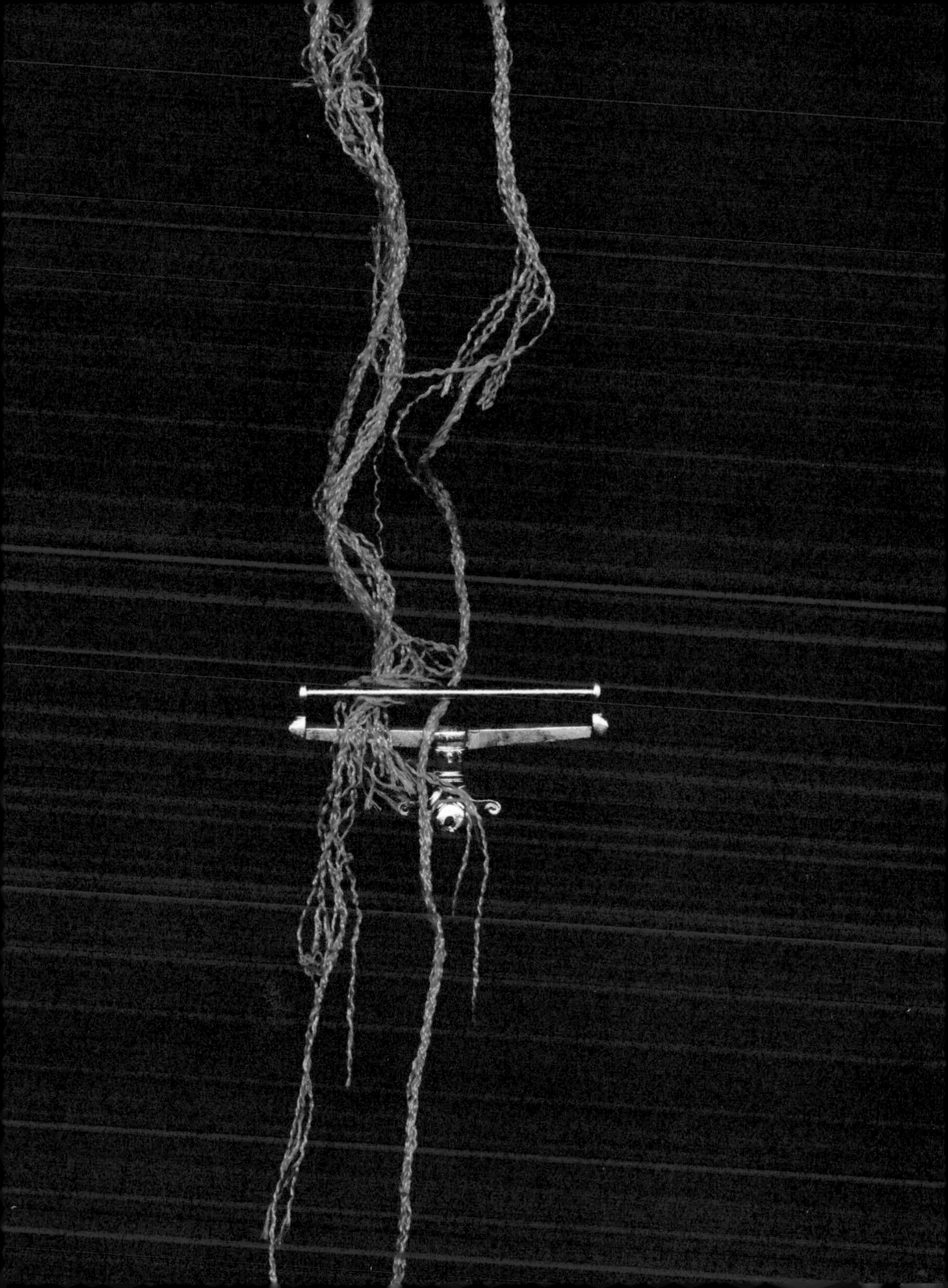

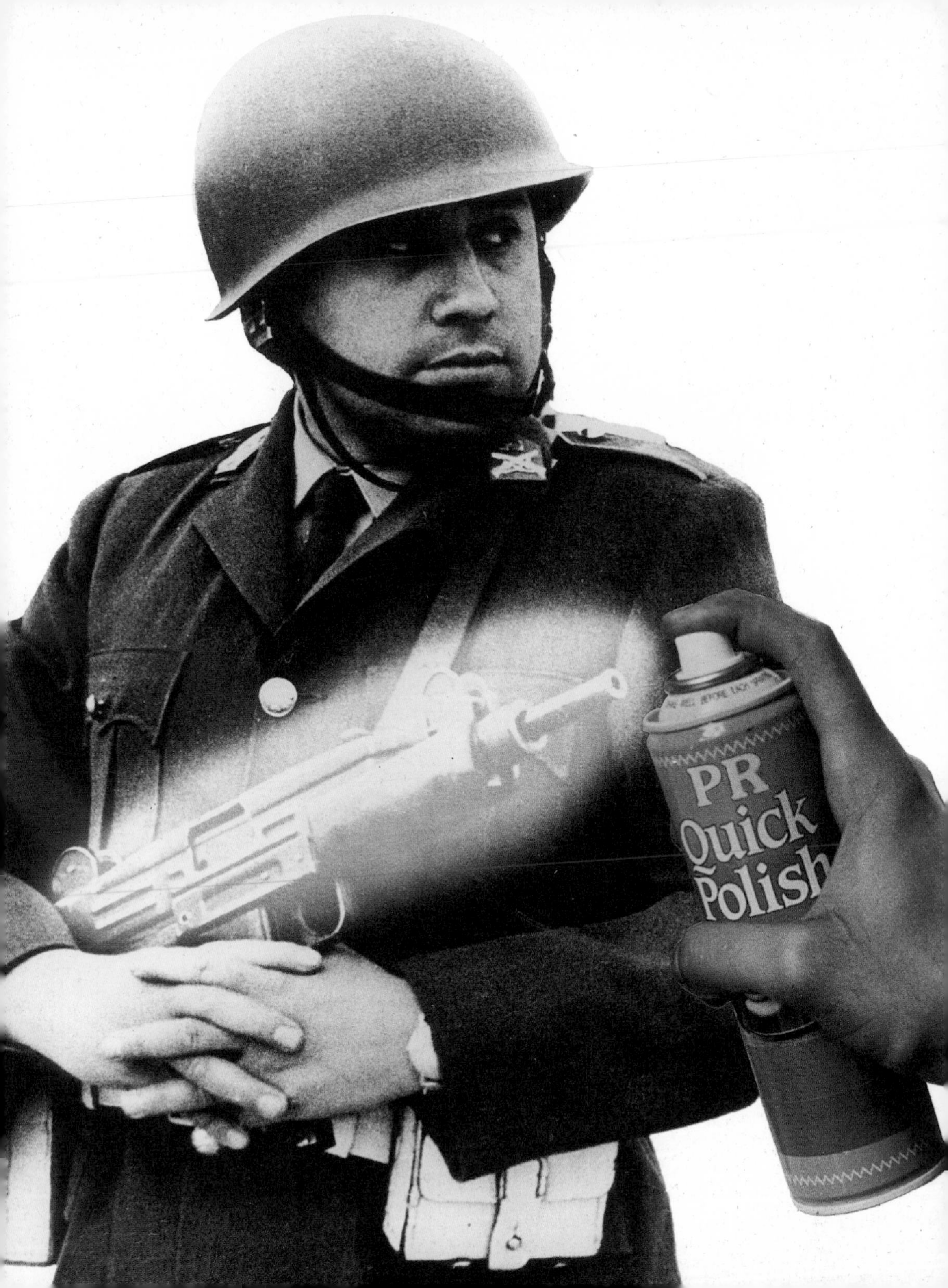
PR
Quick
Polish

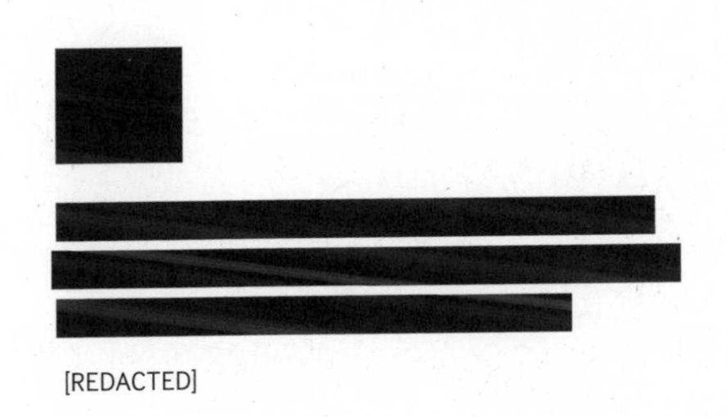
[REDACTED]

## 138000000000

The US government spent $138 billion on private contractors during the invasion and occupation of Iraq

The *Financial Times*

## 95461

In 2010 there were 95,461 registered private military contractors operating in Iraq, compared to 95,900 US military personnel

Congressional Research Service

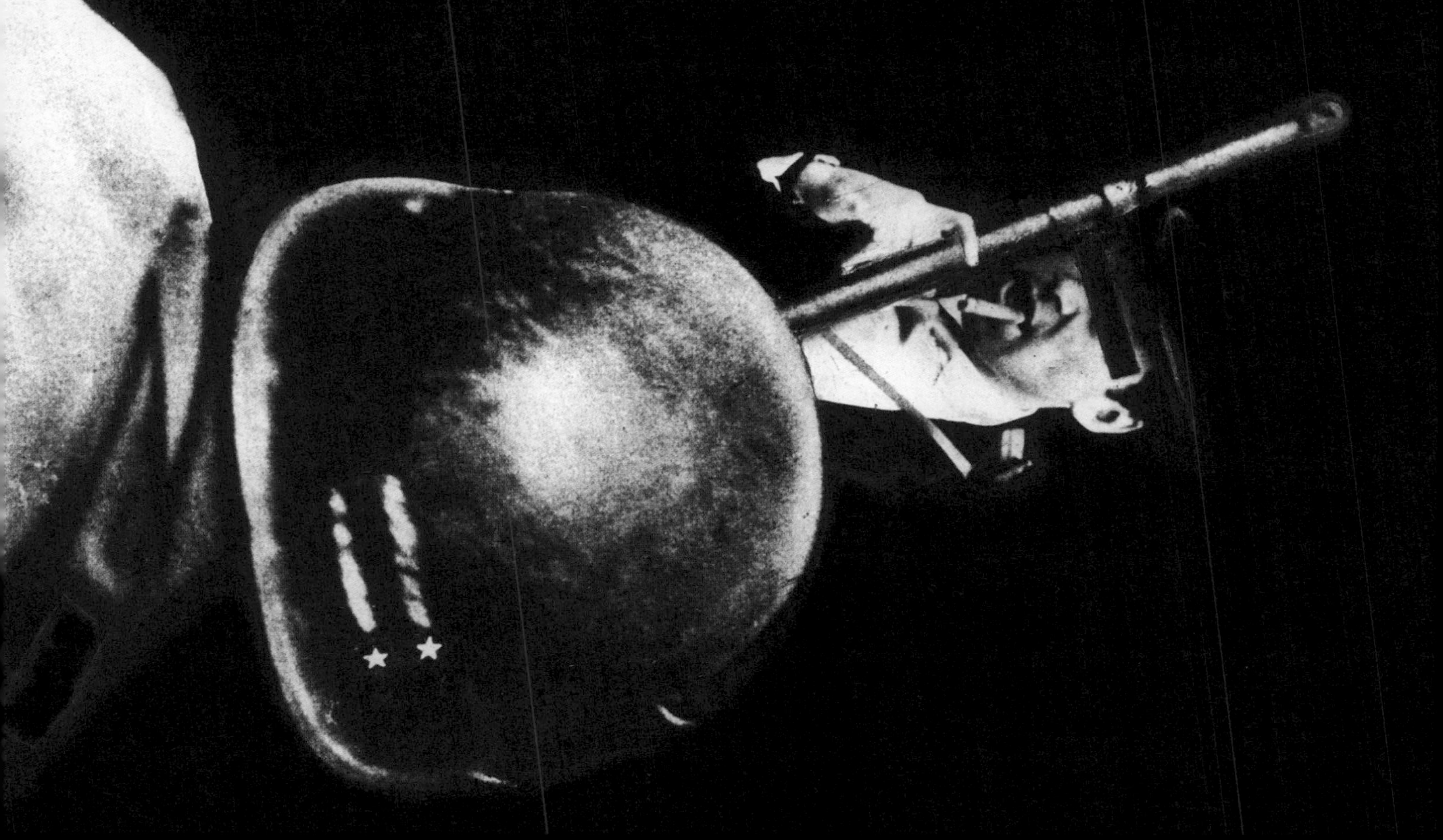

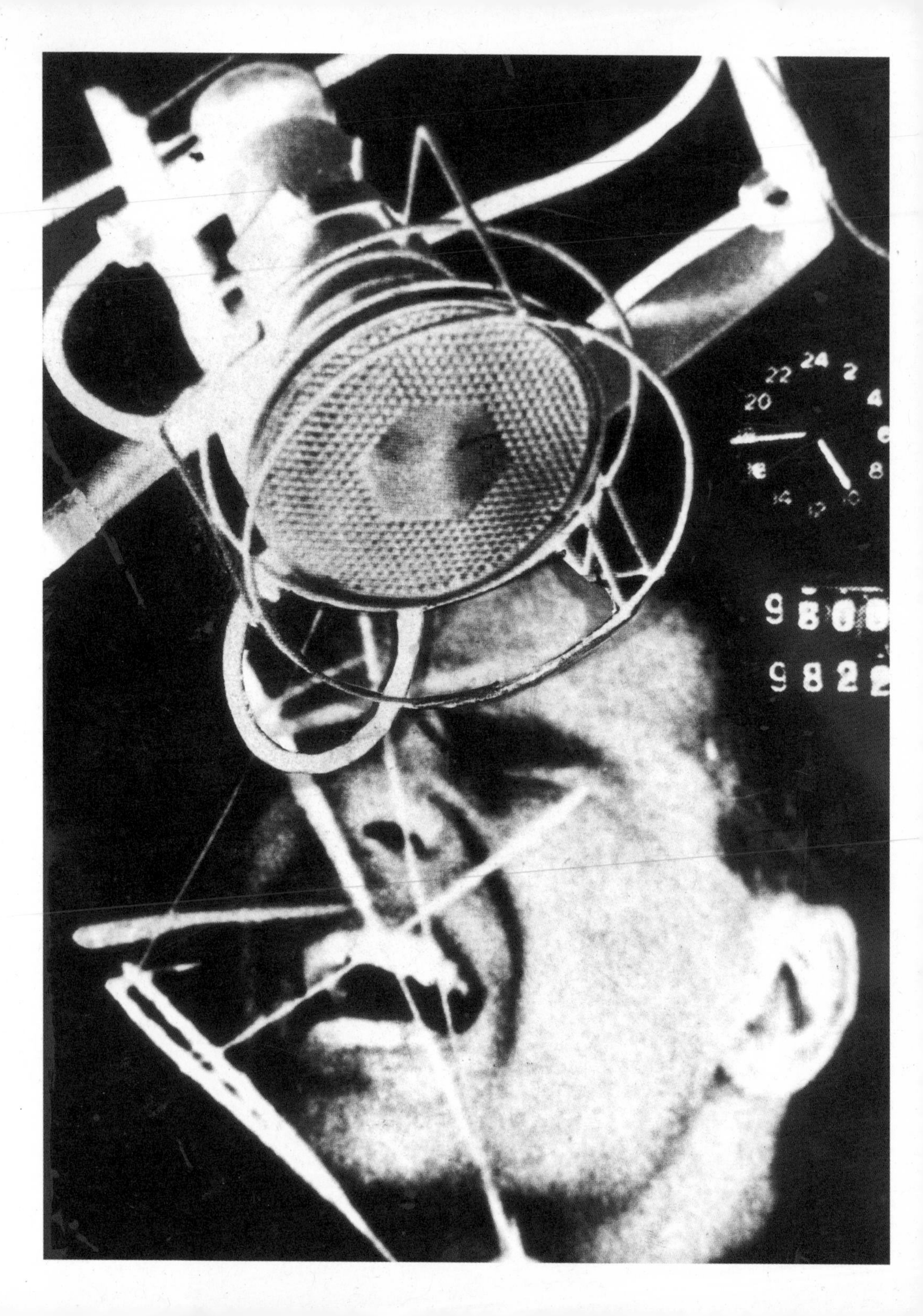
22 24 2
20
4
8
982

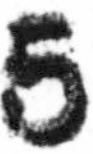

No one shall be subjected to torture or to cruel, inhuman or degrading treatment or punishment

Article 5, Universal Declaration of Human Rights

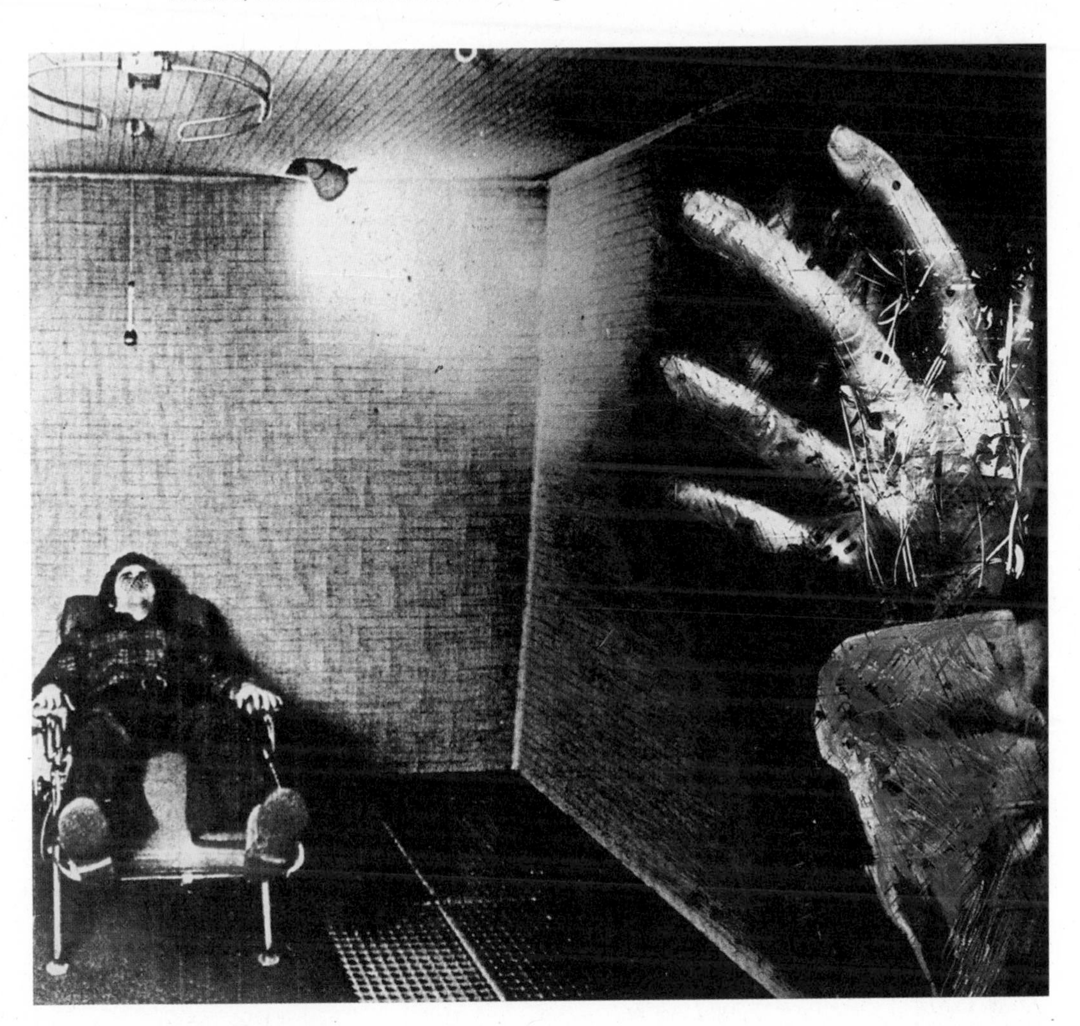

# 122

There were still 122 detainees held without charge by the US government in Guantanamo Bay detention camp in January 2015

Reprieve

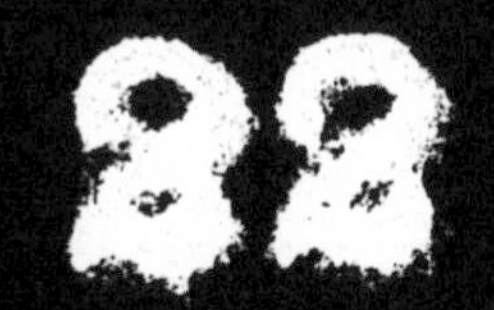

An average of 22 US Army veterans commit suicide every day, 1 every 65 minutes

US Department of Veterans Affairs

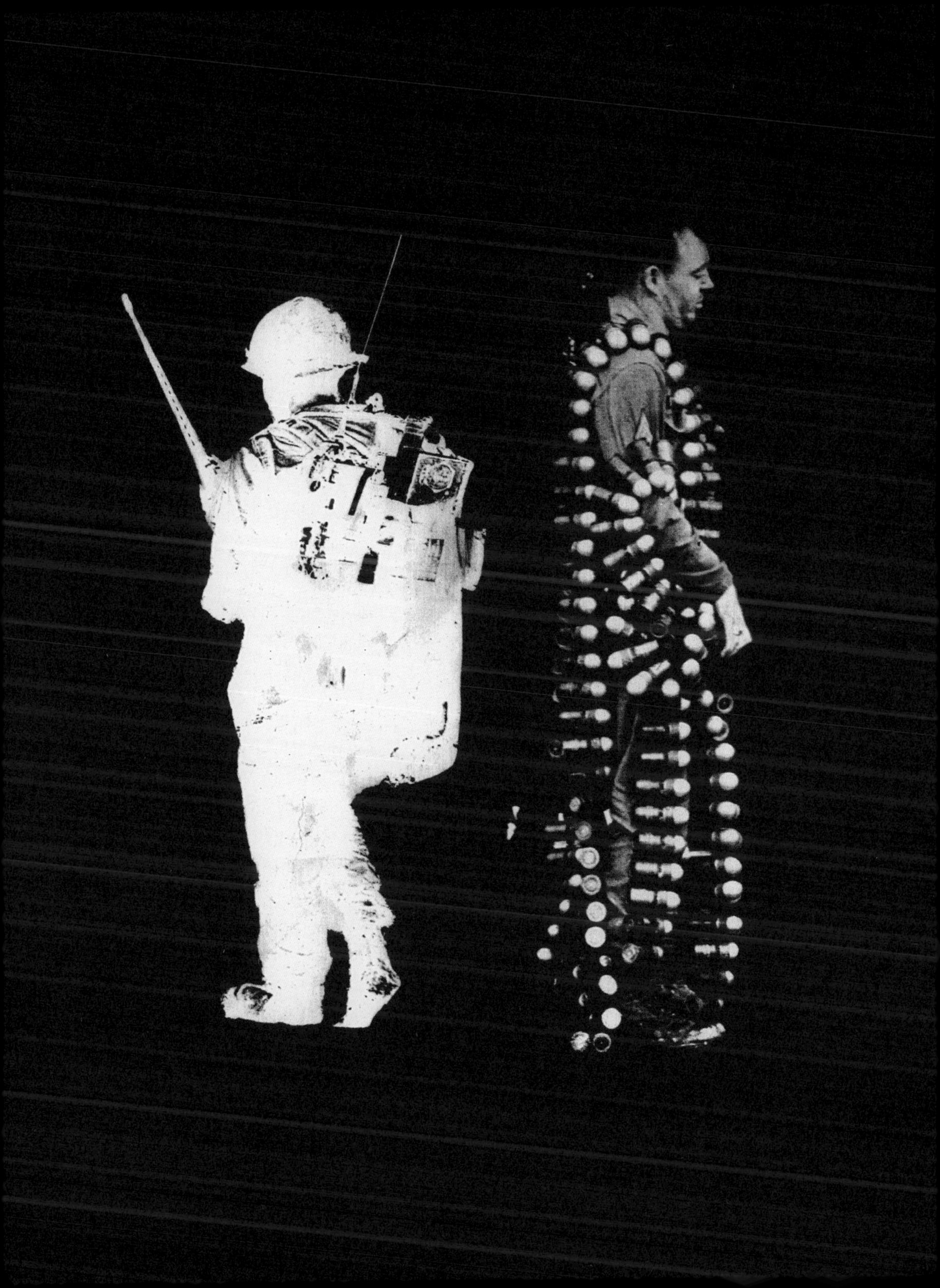

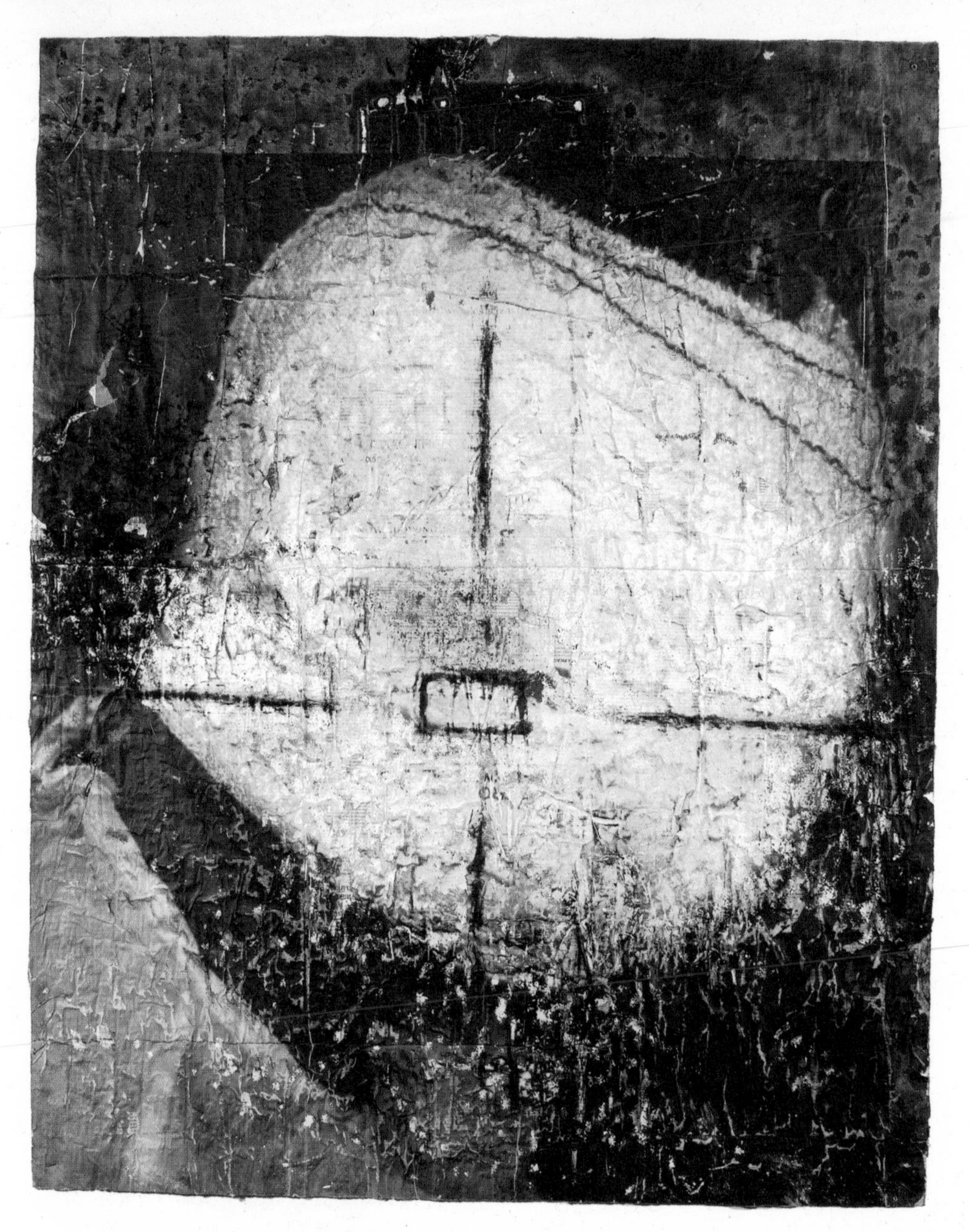

# 1147

In the attempted assassinations of 41 men in Pakistan and Yemen by US drone strikes an estimated 1,147 people were killed, many of whom were women and children

Reprieve

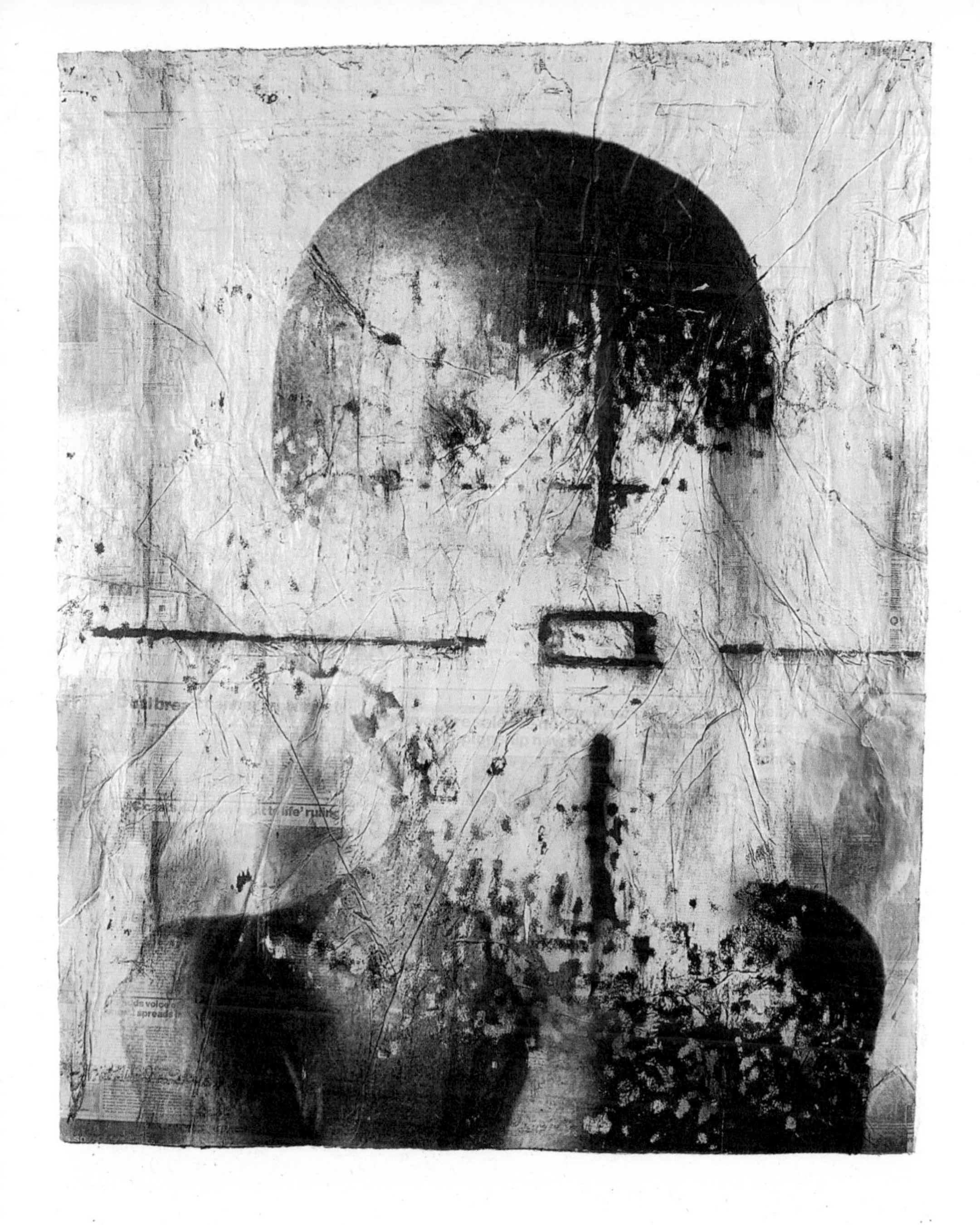

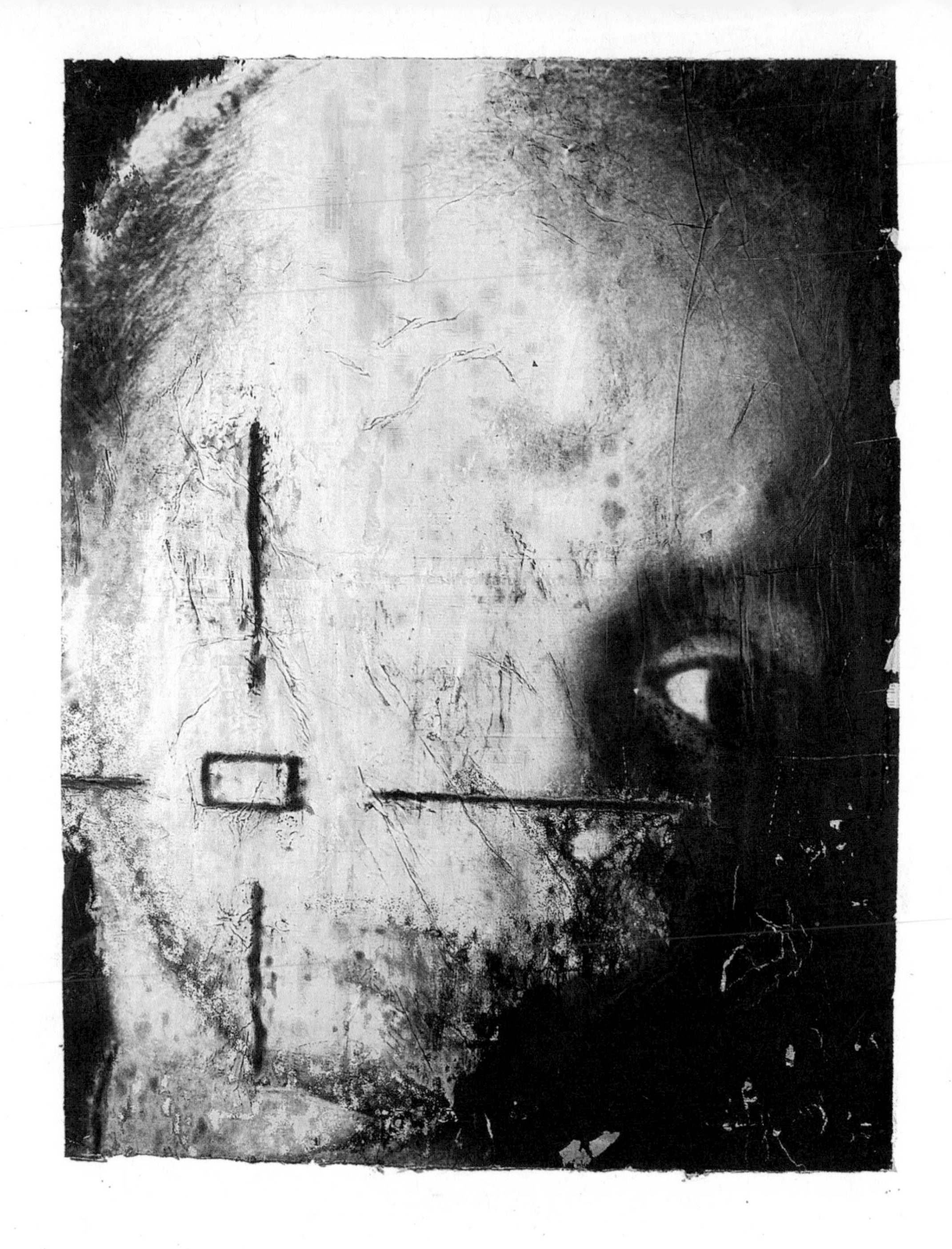

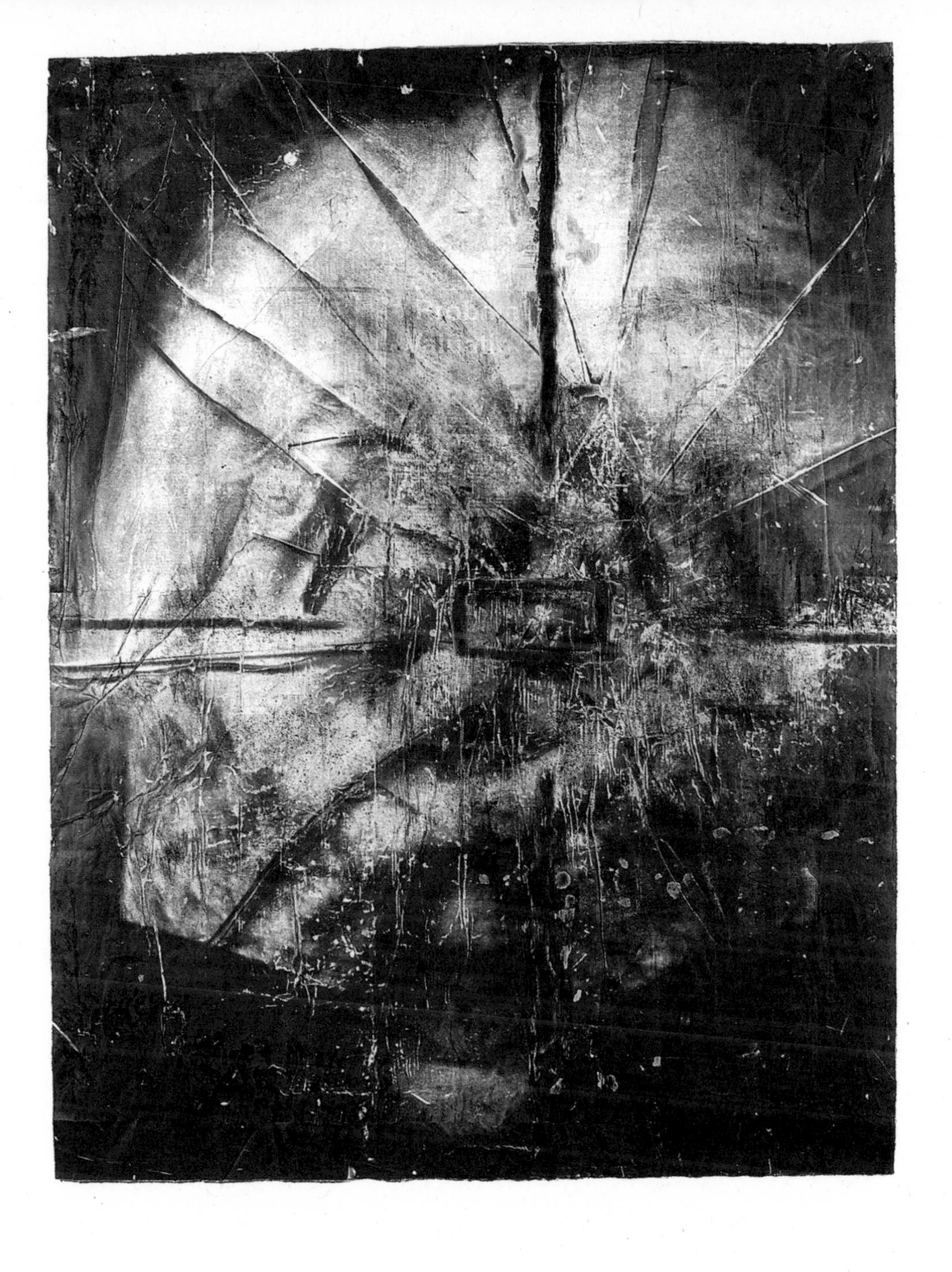

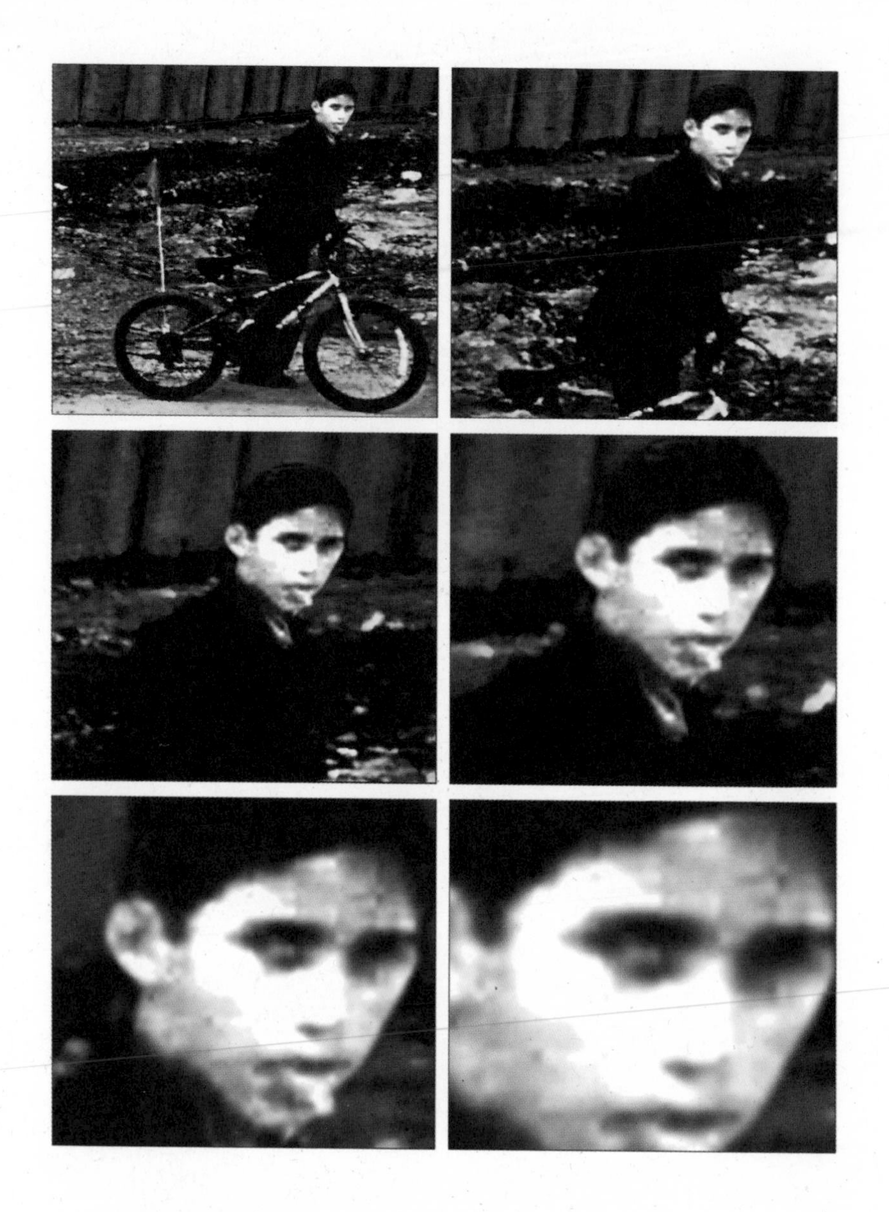

# 71

The number of Israelis killed during the 2014 Gaza War was 71, including 1 child

United Nations Office for the Co-ordination of Humanitarian Affairs

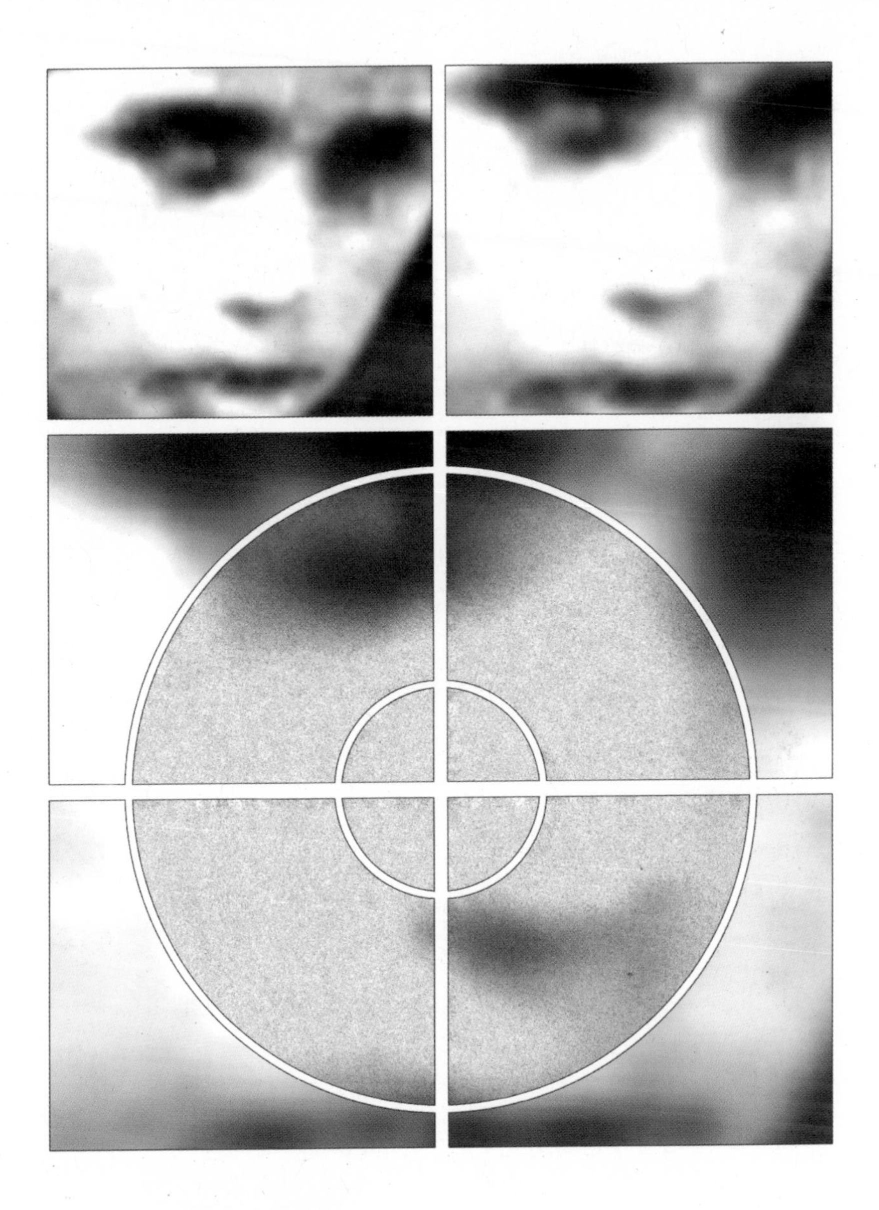

# 2139

The number of Palestinians killed during the 2014 Gaza War was 2,139, including 495 children

United Nations Office for the Co-ordination of Humanitarian Affairs

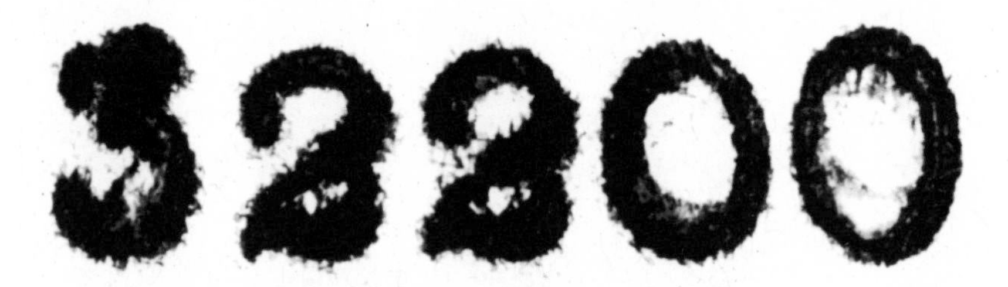


In 2013 an average of 32,200 people per day were forced by conflict and persecution to leave their homes and seek protection, either within the borders of their own country or in other countries. This compares to 23,400 in 2012 and 14,200 in 2011.

The United Nations Refugee Agency

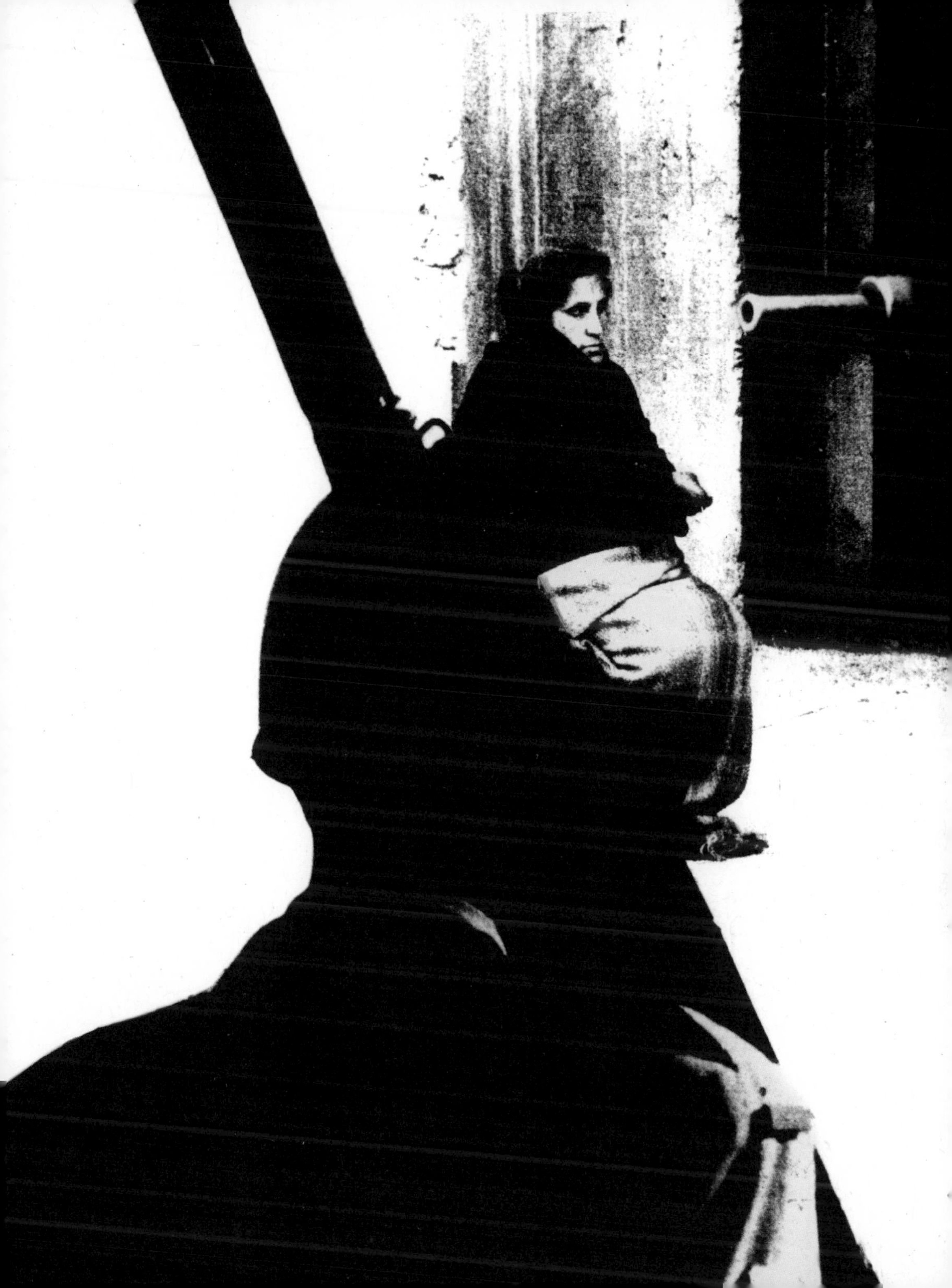

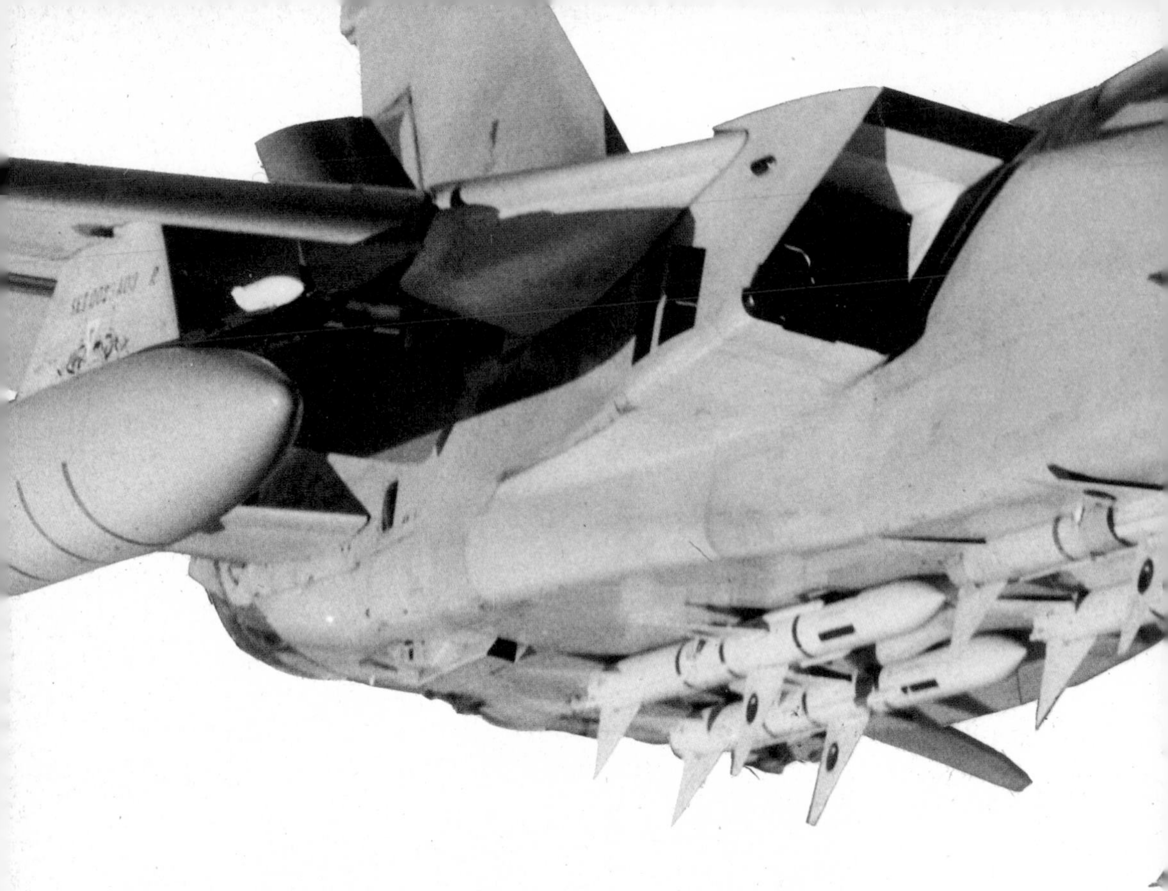

# 9500000

9.5 million Syrians (from a population of 22 million) have fled their homes since the outbreak of civil war in 2011. 3 million have fled Syria and 6.5 million remain internally displaced.

The United Nations Refugee Agency

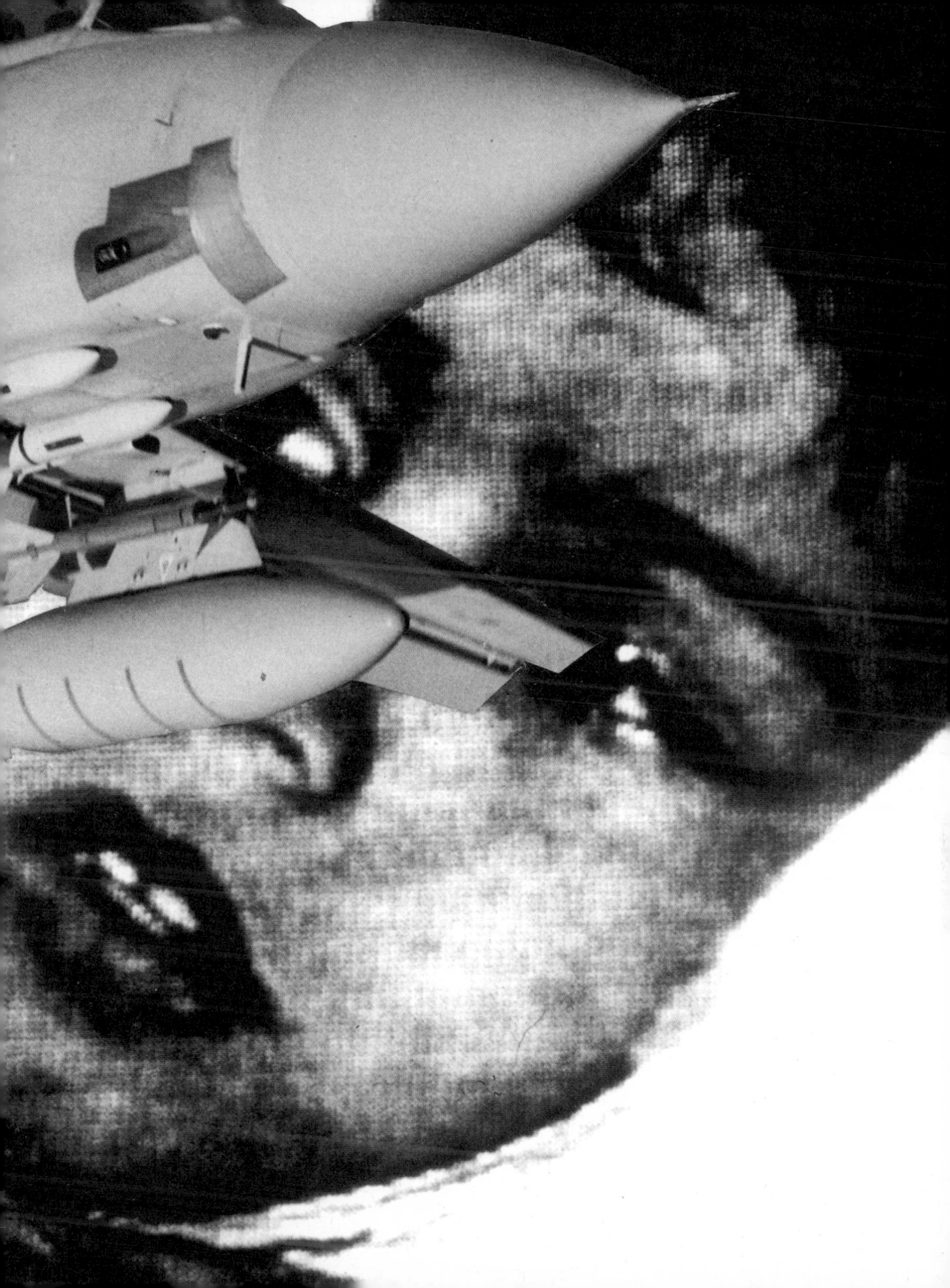

# 3100000

3.1 million children under the age of 5 die due to poor nutrition every year

World Food Programme

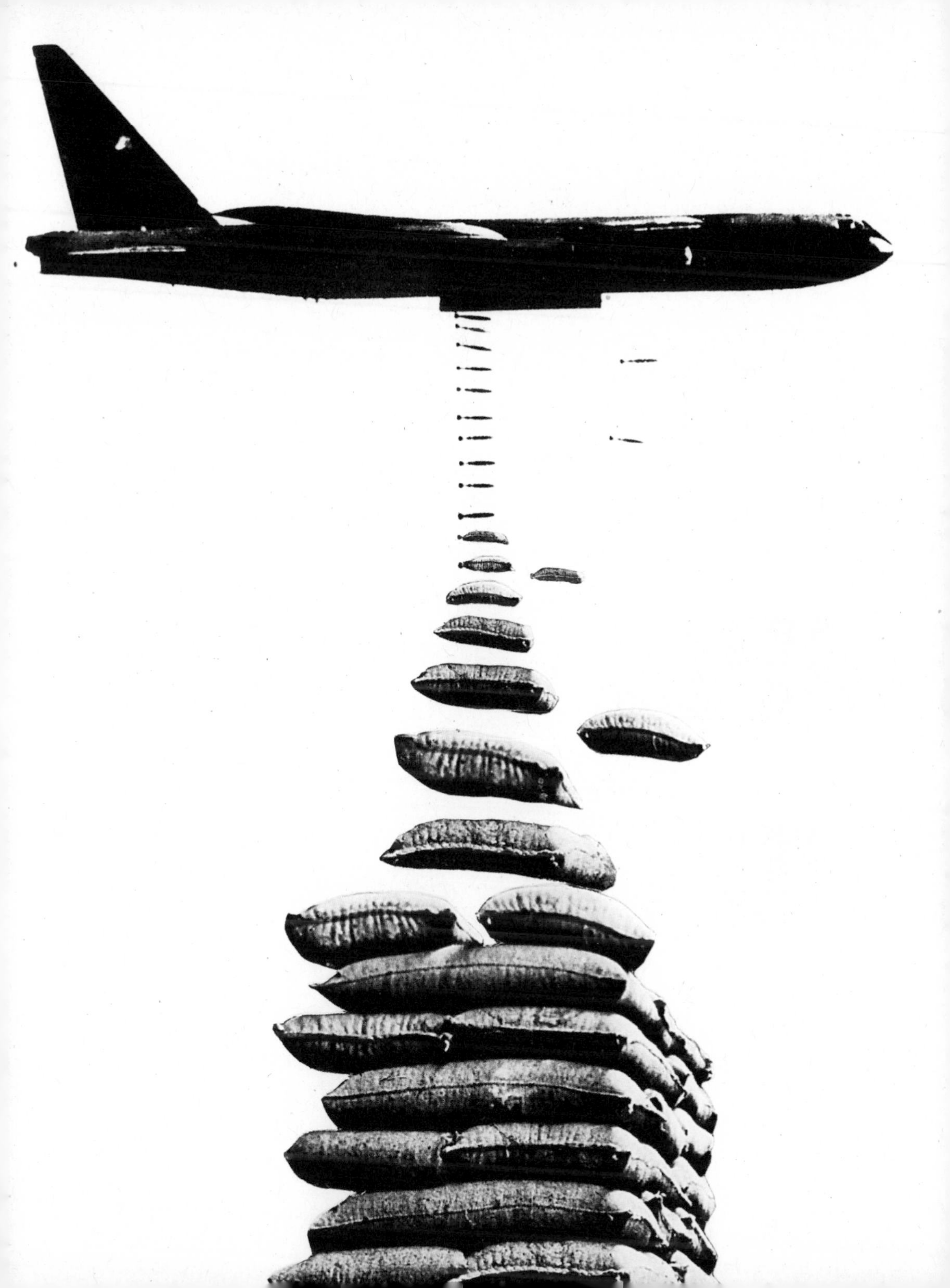

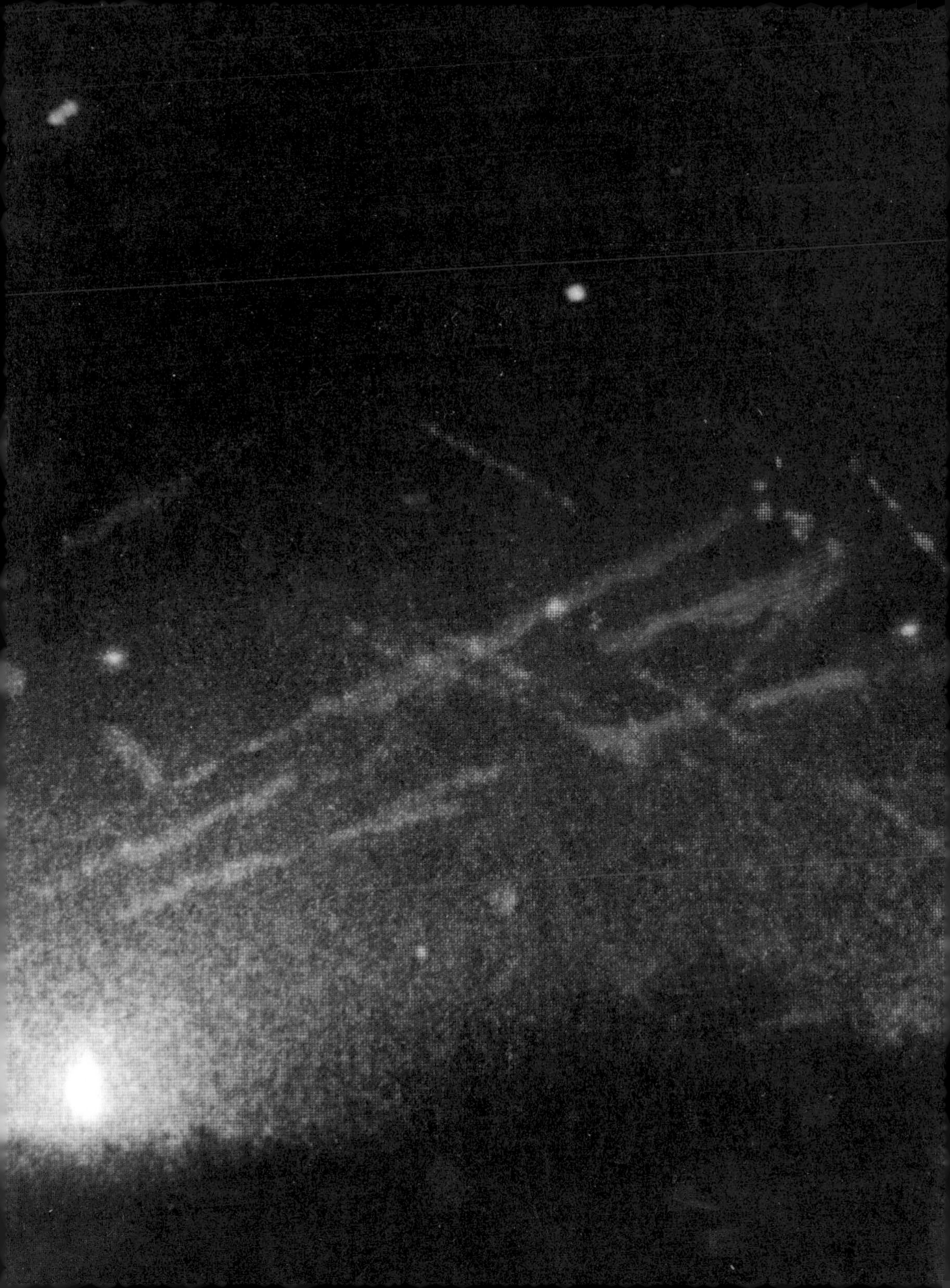

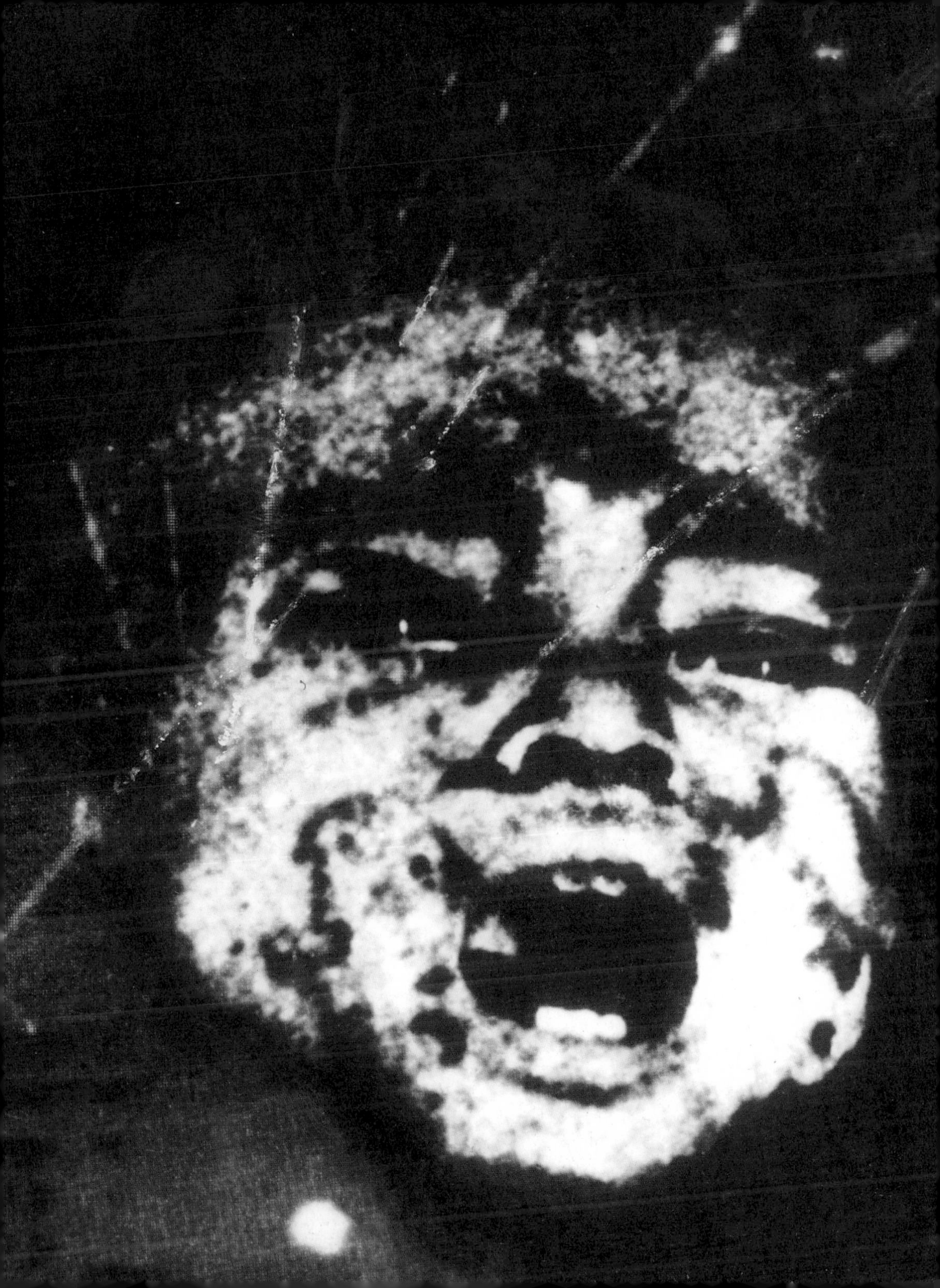

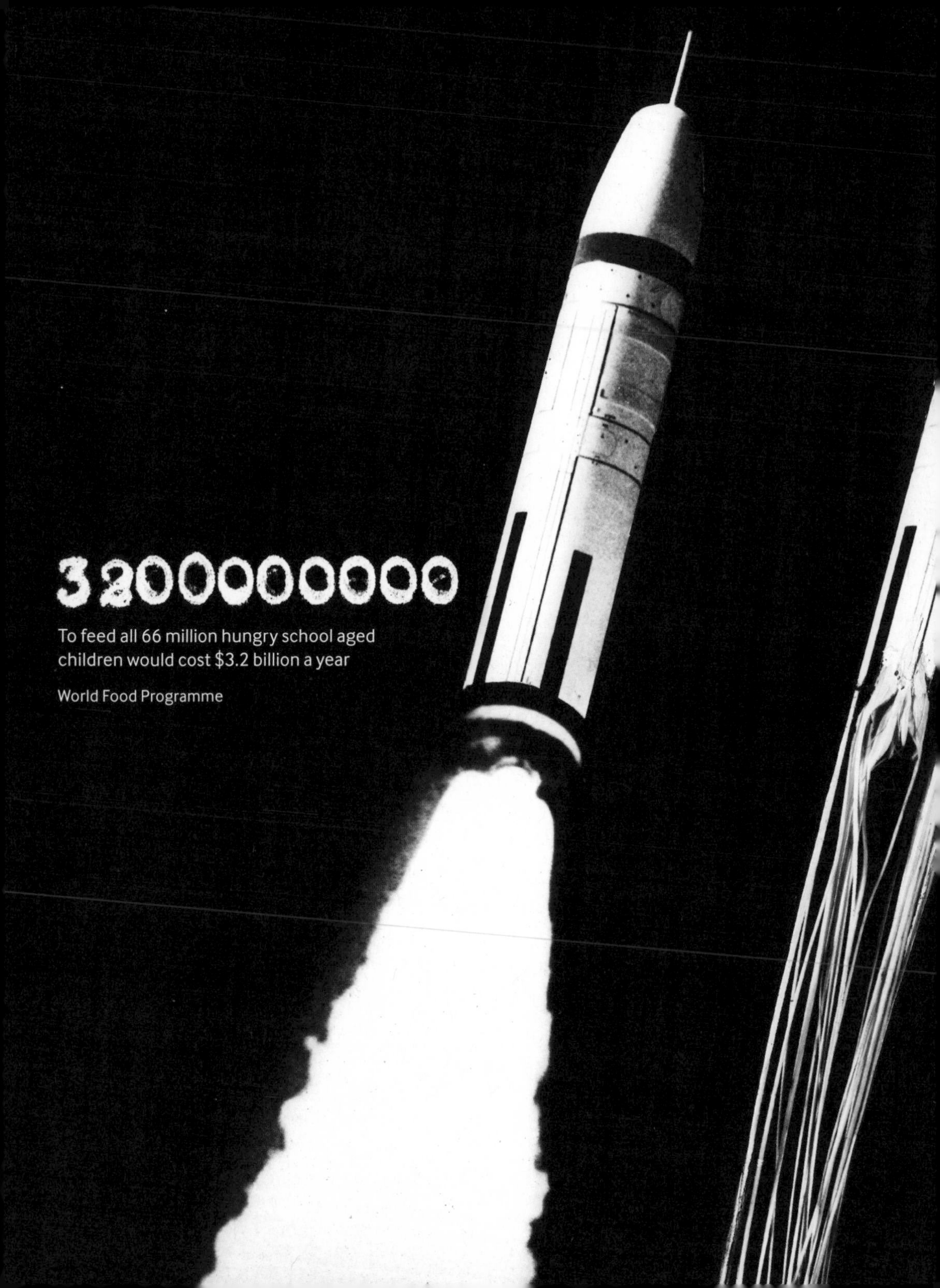
3200000000
To feed all 66 million hungry school aged children would cost $3.2 billion a year
World Food Programme

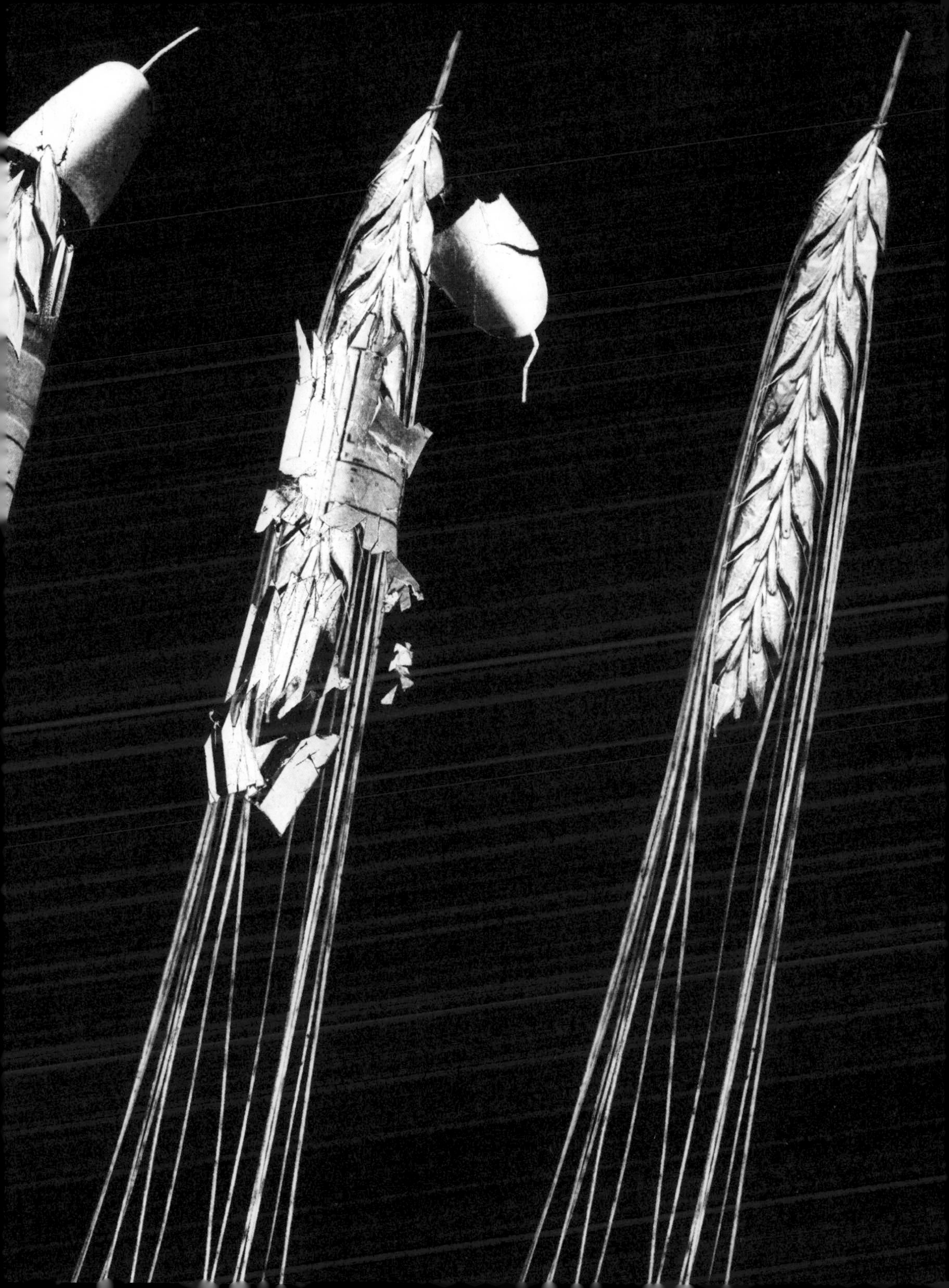

# AFTERWORD / The N0Ose of N0ughts

We live in an alternate reality, an upside down world. The mainstream media feed us a steady drip of concocted scandals, and this anaesthetic dulls us, keeps us passive. We consume stories about a celebrity's 'weight battle' or about a politician going off-message on Twitter.

Most people know something is wrong, that we are missing the real story. At the same time, we are confused. Drowning in this morass of trivia, we feel disorientated. As I walk to my studio, corporate ownership of imagery has slid off the billboards into every crack and crevice of public space. What's on offer is a state of blissless ignorance, intravenously delivered through one of our many screens. The real scandal that our gaze is carefully guided away from – that we are flailing to grab – is the war, poverty and human misery, here and everywhere, that our governments and corporations promote and get rich off. This book is about that scandal.

I have tried to conceptualise this scandal through the use of numbers – numbers that show how we have screwed up. But the numbers in this book are not the usual '45% off Selected Items In-Store' or 'Text 0871-617-0135 for a chance to win an all-inclusive holiday to the Algarve'. The numbers in this book outline, instead, the 94 per cent of revenue the British company BAE Systems reaped from selling military hardware in 2013, or the number of people (1,000,000,000 – one billion) around the world who live on less than a $1 per day.

These are numbers you won't see in a shop front or commercial break. They don't ramp up the 'buying mood'.

The book begins in 1945 with the creation of the United Nations and the atomic bombs dropped on the Japanese cities of Hiroshima and Nagasaki six weeks later. I was born four years after these events and my life has been lived in the shadow of them. This book consists of photomontages and other artwork that I have made from 1968, through the Cold War, up to the present.

I began my working life as a painter, but after those turbulent student protests of 1968 I wanted to find a medium that could relate my work as an artist to my activism. At that time paint as a medium felt to me too weighed down with art history, and I moved into more photo-based work.

As I became active in the anti-Vietnam War movement, photomontage enabled me – by using photos of world events as they actually happened – to make work that could respond directly. London at the time had a vibrant radical press and photomontage as a medium benefitted from the fact that it could be reproduced in newspapers and magazines. I also started to put posters up in the street. When I was an art student in 1972 I fly-posted walls in London with a large photomontage poster I created of a protesting student killed at Kent State University in the US (the image is in this book). It was made and pasted up in the street a few days after the shooting as an act of solidarity. Printed in red water based ink, the image bled in the rain, leaving a blank sheet of paper.

Often, as a Londoner, my work has been about the role of Britain and, because of the close relationship and its superpower status, the role of the United States. We are all implicated in the crimes committed by our own country. I felt from the beginning that it was necessary to focus on my own backyard, so that the work could be used as the visual element in British campaigning and protest. Our country is stacked with nuclear weapons – Britain is one of the five top arms trading countries in the world – and London regularly hosts one of the world's biggest arms fairs.

Most countries are similarly stacked high with weapons, and consequently have anti-war and human rights groups. Therefore, a photomontage which I might create for a British group (for example, the Campaign for Nuclear Disarmament), is soon circulated through newspapers, placards, posters, postcards and the internet, to be used in campaigns globally. At various times, I have returned to painting and made gallery-based installations. For me, it's important to use every possible outlet for my work, from the museum and art gallery to the street and community centre.

The strength of photomontage is the license it gives the artist to make connections that the single click of a camera shutter cannot show. Through photomontage I can engage with the question of how news is constructed and attempt to rip through the veil that separates the images of perpetrator and victim. When I started in the late 1960s that was vital, but now the task is even more crucial as we are bombarded with more and more decontextualised imagery. Photomontage, whether created through the use of cut and paste or digitally, can, I believe, help to make sense of this barrage of anchorless images.

In this book, a photograph of gamblers in a casino is cut together with stock images of missiles, which are transformed into the chips being gambled. The two images become one and in the process create a third, previously hidden meaning. In this case, it could be arms dealers profiting from war, or government ministers and moneymen gambling with the lives of millions of people around the world. Photomontage does not need to be prescriptive – it can allow people to come to their own conclusions by bringing together cause and effect. Images, which previously would otherwise glide in and out of consciousness without a thought, are problematised.

This book supplements this problem with another problem – a number this time, but again decontextualised until the small print is read. The missile/gamblers image, for instance, is juxtaposed with the number 17,27,0. On inspection of the small print, the viewer sees that this was the number of known nuclear weapons in the world in 2013. The gamblers around the card table are gambling with extinction.

Photomontage uses documentary photographs or staged images that are set up. It uses the image bank of daily life to bring about new connections. To emphasise this factual basis, I have included an explanation and source for each of the numbers in the book. The numbers, which are floating with no context over the images, are then brought back to their factual root. Other than where the number is widely agreed and easy to track, as in the case of US and allied deaths in the Vietnam and Iraq wars, the numbers are estimates. But I have used sources whose methodologies have been constructed to get as close as possible to the true number – whether that be the number of Iraqi people killed in the US/UK invasion, or the number of nuclear weapons in the world today. (We only list our own mortalities in wars; we don't officially track the number of people we kill, while countries like Israel and North Korea refuse to be candid about their nuclear weapons capability.)

My goals and methods have not changed radically in the last 40 years. Now, in 2015, working in my studio in Hackney, I am still responding to the world as it floods in via the mass media. With the advent of the internet I have a lot more material to work with, but the issues are still the terrible effect of war, poverty and greed on the peoples of the world. Economic imperialism and war are rampant, as is the rise of terrorism.

Looking back, I realise the seed for the idea of this book was actually planted a quarter of a century ago, at the time of my exhibition *Images for Disarmament* in 1989 at the United Nations in Geneva. I made a speech at the UN to open my exhibition that began with a series of numbers I had heard from Dr Hiroshi Nakajima, Director-General of the World Health Organisation. I recounted in the speech how these numbers had been haunting me. For one billion dollars, he had said, or the cost of just 20 modern military planes, the world could control illnesses that kill 11 million children every year in the developing world.

At that moment, I saw that the connection between children needlessly dying from illness and bloated military spending was concealed in our society; the numbers were kept apart and thus acceptable. But we know deep down that such equations, and there are too many like them, are in fact the matrix of numbers that are the foundation of our modern world. Somehow, mainly with the helping hand of a corrupted media, we learn to live with it, we learn to keep the numbers apart, we learn to keep our conscience clean. Somehow we accept, or push out of our brains, the fact that in our world, 20 military planes that rain death are more important than the lives of 11 million sick children. We can live with that. Can we?

My art seeks to make these equations impossible to live with. My photomontage attempts to scramble this matrix of numbers – to rip apart the smooth, bleached, and apparently seamless surface of the media's presentation of the world and to expose the conflict and grubby reality underneath.

Twenty-five years after I gave that speech at the UN, the numbers that indict our world are worse than before. More money is spent on arms, more people are displaced by war and conflict, climate catastrophe is already affecting millions of people, and more children die of preventable diseases.

The laces of noughts that run through this book form the noose with which we are killing ourselves and each other. But, as in photomontage, with slight manipulation, these noughts are instead links in a chain – a chain of protestors and resistors refusing to accept the nightmarish calculus we are endlessly told is inevitable.

**Peter Kennard**
2015

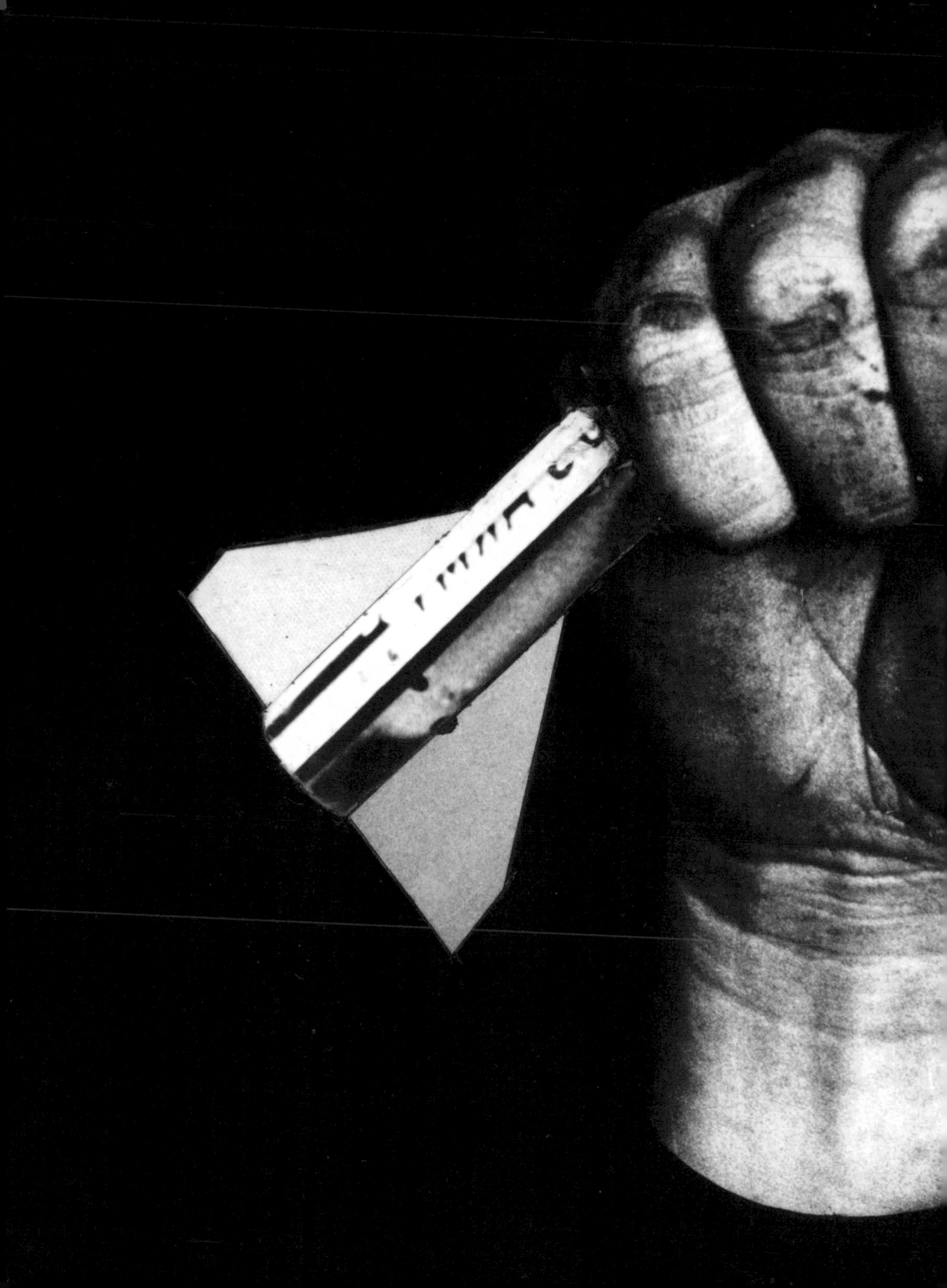